MIDLIFE RENEWAL

Dedication

To my friends, colleagues and acquaintances, who generously opened their hearts to talk about the difficult times of midlife.

Copyright © KR Publishing and James Forson

All reasonable steps have been taken to ensure that the contents of this book do not, directly or indirectly, infringe any existing copyright of any third person and, further, that all quotations or extracts taken from any other publication or work have been appropriately acknowledged and referenced. The publisher, editors and printers take no responsibility for any copyright infringement committed by an author of this work.

Copyright subsists in this work. No part of this work may be reproduced in any form or by any means without the written consent of the publisher or the author.

While the publisher, editors and printers have taken all reasonable steps to ensure the accuracy of the contents of this work, they take no responsibility for any loss or damage suffered by any person as a result of that person relying on the information contained in this work.

First published in 2018

ISBN: 978-1-86922-741-8 (Printed)
ISBN: 978-1-86922-742-5 (ePDF)

Published by KR Publishing
P O Box 3954
Randburg
2125
Republic of South Africa

Tel: (011) 706-6009
Fax: (011) 706-1127
E-mail: orders@knowres.co.za
Website: www.kr.co.za

Printed and bound: Tandym Print, 1 Park Road, Western Province Park, Epping, 7475
Typesetting, layout and design: Cia Joubert, cia@knowres.co.za
Cover design: Marlene de Villiers, marlene@knowres.co.za
Editing and proofreading: Valda Strauss: valda@global.co.za
Project management: Cia Joubert, cia@knowres.co.za

MIDLIFE RENEWAL

Unlock the Hidden Door

A practical conversation about creating a
fulfilling and contented second half

Including twenty practical activities to create a new you

by

James Forson

With a Chapter on 'Your Brain and Midlife'
by Sam Mphuthi
Registered Clinical Psychologist
Neuropsychology and Medico-Legal Practice
M.Sc. (Clin.Psy), B.Soc.Sc (Hons)

2018

"Renewal can take you to places you don't expect!"
— *Sam Mphuthi*

Table of Contents

About the author iv
Prologue vi

1 Introduction 1

    1.1 Why do you need to do this? 2
    1.2 What we are NOT going to deal with 4
    1.3 Living a life of significance 5
    1.4 Some thoughts for what lies ahead 8
    1.5 An overview of your journey 9
    1.6 A quick summary 10

2 Change 15

    2.1 Understanding change 16
    2.2 Summary 26

3 Your Brain and Midlife 27

    3.1 Introduction 28
    3.2 Simplified anatomy of the brain and its functions 30
    3.3 Physically changing the brain through learning and renewal (change) 37
    3.4 Linking one's brain functioning to renewal 40
    3.5 Conclusion 44

4	Midlife	47
	4.1 Time to step back	49
	4.2 Taking stock	50
	4.3 Summary	51
	4.4 Case Study: Richard the banker	51
5	Evaluation	55
	5.1 Creating your own life timeline	57
	5.2 Life ambitions	62
	5.3 The 'Circle of Influence'	66
	5.4 Summary	68
	5.5 Case Study: Sandra – afraid to jump!	70
6	Exploration	73
	6.1 What is your Happiness Base?	74
	6.2 Exploring the unknown	77
	6.3 Finding the connections	79
	6.4 Summary	81
	6.5 Case Study: Simphiwe the entrepreneur	82
7	Consolidation	85
	7.1 Pulling it together	87
	7.2 Impact on your immediate circle	90
	7.3 For love or money?	90
	7.4 Training and preparation	91
	7.5 The Big Decision	94
	7.6 Summary	94
	7.7 Case Study: Creative Lindiwe	95
8	Planning and Empowering	99
	8.1 Where to start?	100
	8.2 What do you need?	104
	8.3 The support team	105

	8.4 Compromises	106
	8.5 Building resilience	107
	8.6 Summary	110
	8.7 Case Study: Annemarie the reframer	110
9	Action	115
	9.1 The Launch	116
	9.2 Keeping on track	118
	9.3 Summary	118
10	Epilogue	121
	10.1 Leave something of value	122
11	Index of Activities	124

Resources 125
Personal support for your own journey 125
Quotations 125
The Transition Model 125
The Burning Platform 126
Building Resilience 126
Kotter's 8-Step Process 126
Lewin's Change Management Model 126
The Minimalists 127
Brain Pickings 127
On Being 127
List of Adjectives 129
List of Resources 131
References 131

About the Author

James Forson spends a great deal of time near the centre of an intricate Venn diagram where management consulting, fiction and business writing, social investment, governance, home-grown vegetables and procrastination overlap. James is a latecomer to writing. It was sparked by writing a biography of his father for a family history. He found that he was full of stories that had to see the light of day. He attended school in Worcester, South Africa, where his initial love of books was fostered. He studied further at the University of Cape Town and was dragged into the world of business with work experience in the mining, steel, pharmaceutical and banking industries.

For the past 24 years he has been an independent management consultant working with clients across a broad range of industries and environments. In the course of his consulting practice, he has worked with a number of executives who have expressed dissatisfaction with their lives. This is where his interest in midlife renewal was awakened, as he counselled and supported his clients to live more humanly rewarding lives. He has taken the tools, methods and concepts he used and developed, and has created a book to assist folk dealing with the complexity and anxiety of midlife renewal.

He is married to Merle and they have an adult son, Tim. They live in Johannesburg.

James likes to say that he knows very little about a great many things.

Other works from James Forson:

Remembering Ramosa: A biography of Robert Forson
Wooden Overcoat: The story of the Drakensberg Air Service
[editor]
Letters from Lonehill: A book of short stories
Bright Shadows: An action novel
Butterflies in the Breeze: A collection of poetry

james.forson@mweb.co.za
http://jamesforsonwriter.wordpress.com/
www.jamesforson.com

Prologue

In my day job as a management consultant, I meet people from all sorts of backgrounds, and we get to know each other, albeit for only short periods of time. In the course of general conversation, I have discovered that many of us – in midlife – are uncomfortable with our situation. While we speak about it at great length, we usually cannot fully comprehend its implications because we are immersed in the present life stage. Our perspectives are subjective, making it difficult to take a broader, more balanced view of life. It was during this time that my own midlife crisis came and went, after which I researched the concept of midlife and renewal and, in a circuitous, serendipitous manner, came up with the concept of a midlife renewal process. In spite of several delays, mainly due to having to earn a living, I was constantly reminded that many people are desperate for information and advice on dealing with this difficult time of readjustment. My research slowed for a number of years.

In 2015, after I had published a book of short stories, *Letters from Lonehill*, I asked myself: why not put down all my thoughts and ideas on midlife renewal in book form, and make it more accessible to anyone who required it? It seems so obvious now, but at the time, it was a breakthrough for me.

My grateful thanks go to Louis van der Merwe, Marie McCrae and Rod Warner, who read early drafts of the book and provided much-needed insights and improvements. Jackie Erasmus and Simone le Hane were wonderful in assisting with the case studies. Jane Theron of Crystal Communications transformed the early text and made the document readable. This book would not have seen the light of day without the valuable insights and encouragement of Sam Mphuthi. Our working relationship goes back beyond a decade during which we worked together on some truly challenging assignments. Furthermore, we have solved many of the world's problems at our coffee hangout in Bryanston. Not only has Sam written the chapter on rewiring the brain – a crucial part of what renewal aims to achieve – but he has been critical, demanding and supportive in just the right ratios.

My wife Merle unconditionally continues to support my writing addiction in good spirits.

In your hand is the finished product. I hope you will get in touch with me to share your successes and achievements. Your comments will help to improve the book in future editions. It is my fervent hope that the contents will be of great assistance to you as you live out the rest of your life with joy and contentment.

James Forson
January 2018

Chapter 1
Introduction

The first step toward change is awareness.
The second step is acceptance.
— Nathaniel Branden

If you are in midlife and have a growing awareness that your situation is uncomfortable, this book is for you. You want something more in life, or want something different. You have that nagging feeling that you should make some significant changes in your life, but don't know what they are. You want something better to look forward to – the excitement back again. But where to start? With so many outside demands on you, your time and your finances, you just don't have time for yourself.

You are trying to find the door leading to a more fulfilling life, but are dragged back to the constant responsibilities of work and relationships. That door is open, but you need to search for it. This book provides insights and exercises to help you make the mental connections, and take you to the important decisions that you must confront in this phase of your life. It is crucial that you find that door yourself. It is there, it is open. You simply need to see it.

This midlife uncertainty is uncomfortable. It fills you with a gnawing concern that somehow you are missing out. Everybody else around you seems to be living a purposeful, high-achieving life, and you are wallowing in drudgery. We spend the early part of our adult lives building a career, building a family or support structures around us; we become so bound up in the boredom of day-to-day survival that when we get those things sorted during this phase, we feel let down and disappointed.

1.1 Why do you need to do this?

Perhaps you bought this book because the topic resonates with your own midlife questions. Let's examine the reasons.

- You are in midlife, and that can mean any age from 40 to 65 years old.
- You feel stuck, bored or directionless.
- Your career has taken you somewhere other than where you wanted to go when you started out.

- You are on the treadmill of work, sleep and family[i] commitments.
- Your career is currently on track, but you don't like where you are now.

Make any connections? If your answers are mainly yes, then you are in the right place; we are going to work this out together, and believe me, you are not alone.

You may also have experienced warnings that your mortality is finite. A heart murmur, a frightening growth, a persistent pain can bring home the savage realisation that you are not going to last forever. These warnings can be devastating, but they will also propel you into new directions, nudging you towards that open door.

In midlife, your career has usually stabilised to a predictable trajectory. Your family and personal relationships are settling into a comfortable pattern. You have built up career expertise, and you have found a niche for yourself. This is not to say you haven't or won't swop jobs or life partners, but equilibrium has been reached.

Midlife is also a time of serenity, a time of joy, and a time of greater personal maturity and acceptance. It is not about achieving great things for public acclaim. It is about living a life of meaning. Great achievement with no meaning is pointless. Being a CEO of a global firm is pointless if your wife or husband has left you, your children detest you, and your friends avoid you. A good midlife sets us up for a good old age.

---

i   There are many different forms of social unit and the modern family has evolved beyond the patriarchal, nuclear concept of a father, mother and children. We all live in families of one sort or another. I do not exclude families with no children or same sex parent families, or single parent families or single persons living alone. All these are special families. I refer to families mainly in the traditional sense; it is not to exclude other families, but is done so for the sake of brevity and to avoid repetition.

A balanced midlife allows us to live lives of significance.

Take Action Now!

Activity 1 – Reasons for Midlife Renewal

Make a list of all the reasons why you are currently considering a midlife renewal. They could involve relationships, situations or responsibilities. Consider the linkages between the thoughts you have captured. Try to find a recurring pattern behind your notes.

1.2 What we are NOT going to deal with

Let's clarify what we are *not* going to deal with in this book so that you can focus on your expectations. There is a formidable task ahead!

We are not going to deal with depression, or midlife crisis, or the fallout from divorce or retrenchment. These are specialist subjects and there are many excellent resources and services that address these concerns. If you have experienced something pathological and traumatic, my best advice is to seek support from the appropriate specialists or professionals. Go and do it now.

1.3 Living a life of significance

We all want to live a life of significance. We want to be taken seriously. We want to be people of value. But to whom should our lives be significant? Should one's life's be significant to other people, so that we can garner admiration and approval? Or should it be a quieter, more reflective, inner sort of significance?

For much of our lives we focus on planning, achieving and becoming. We want to be someone. We want to be esteemed. We want people to think well of us. We want respect, and so we put our lives together in a way that we hope will give us that. And for many of us, in our early years, success, material gain, wealth, power and significance are synonymous.

Chapter 1: Introduction

We want to leave a legacy. Something that will live on after us, which will remind people of what wonderful people we were. But, in the course of doing so, we lose not only other people of value, but sometimes we lose ourselves. A legacy can only be enjoyed after our death. Why live for something that will only be received after we no longer exist? If we want to leave a legacy, our focus is on creating something that will live on after us. It is not about living a significant life right now, in our current circumstances.

As we get older, and perhaps wiser, we find that success, our personal inner success, has a different dimension. We realise that there will always be people who have a bigger house, a more expensive car, or a bigger salary. We have discovered that if we try to go after these material things, once we have them, they no longer satisfy us. An adequate house has to give way to a more extravagant house. A challenging, rewarding job has to give way to a job with a more impressive title and better earnings. We believe this to be our entitlement.

In this view of the world, our value as human beings comes down to the size of our TV screen, the engine capacity of our motor car and the size of the corporate budgets we control.

And we have to work hard to maintain them. That next promotion, that next job change, that new purchase, that expensive foreign cruise, come at great human cost. We neglect friends, family and others significant to us as we struggle to reach this ever-receding goal.

We develop impressive five-year and ten-year personal plans. We glowingly describe what we consider to be that coveted end state of our lives. And the attention is more on what we will own, what we will have, and less on whom we will be. But being successful is not the same as being significant.

Of course, none of these things are bad in and of themselves. They make us into important human beings. It's just that we should not delude ourselves that chasing after these things makes us into significant humans.

Living a life of significance comes down to meaning and value. It's about the meaning we attach to our own lives. It's about the way we value ourselves.

Let's approach this from a different angle. Think about what your family, friends and colleagues will say about you a week after your funeral has taken place. What are the 'you-shaped' dents you have left in the world? Your friends aren't going to speak admiringly about your lovely home, your expensive car or the large estate you left behind. They won't talk about the long hours at work, or your promotions. They will be talking about your significance. Some of the things they will mention may be your sense of humour. Your kindness. Your gift for music. Your patience. Your skill at woodwork or repairing broken appliances. Your disarming blush. Your magnificent bread-and-butter pudding. The tea cosies you knitted and shared as gifts. The many times you encouraged your children or cheered up a neighbour.

These are the real significant achievements.

Take a moment to think about people who hold a special significance for you. Differentiate between people you admire and people with significance. Who are they? Why are they significant? What about them do you respect?

You may admire someone for running a large multi-national company or for climbing five of the highest mountain peaks in the world, but is this person of significance to you? Significant people are much more likely to be in your inner circle: a parent, a friend, a teacher. Something about their behaviour has made an impression on you. They expressed an unconditional interest in you; they let you know that you were someone special and expected nothing in return.

Think about this last sentence:

They expressed an unconditional interest in you; they let you know that you were someone special and expected nothing in return.

Chapter 1: Introduction

As a person in midlife, you know that your life will come to an end. You are unlikely to know when, but inwardly you know that you have probably lived for more days than the days you have yet to live. Your life will come to an end.

Regardless of your religious beliefs or if you have no religious beliefs at all, the universe does not owe you anything. What you have is what you have now. Any significance you have as a human being, you have to go out and acquire for yourself.

And this changes our internal narrative – that little voice that is constantly talking to us. Our narrative changes to reflecting about living a life others will want to emulate. Our emphasis here is on life, not lifestyle. With enough money anybody can have a desirable lifestyle. A desirable life, worthy of copying, is another matter. A desirable lifestyle will fill your life with things that others may consider prised or enviable. But it will be hollow and unfulfilling if you have not created a life of significance.

A life worthy of emulation embraces an emphasis on people rather than things. After all, things are just that – things. You know how you have gone out shopping after payday, and brought home that wonderful something that caught your eye. And two days later, it has lost its lustre. It has just become another thing in a cupboard. People, on the other hand, continue to surprise, entertain and sometimes disappoint you. Whatever their circumstance in your life, they can never be relegated to a cupboard.

On the day that we die, all our wealth and possessions are immediately transferred to someone else. Sometimes not even to the people mentioned in our will. They may destroy or sell things we cherished, and value things we thought worthless. And even if we get to pick where our earthly goods go, the reality is that the recipient is always someone other than us.

Success is never enough. Financial success will never satisfy the innermost desires of our soul. No matter the amount of financial success earned, it always leaves us wanting more. Significance always lasts. Even when you are no longer present, your significance will still be yours. And nothing can ever take that away from you.

Midlife is a time to reconsider what that significance is. We have an opportunity to remodel ourselves. To make good the errors of our past. And be more congruent with the significant human being we want to be.

Know that your life is a work in progress. The things you do, the beliefs you have, are open to and should remain open to reflection and change. Our lives and the way we live them are constantly being built up and broken down. Sometimes we are in a good place and sometimes in a very bad place. We do the best we can to survive. Our human society very often won't make sense. Become comfortable with that. Let us commit to being significant as we rework the clay of our lives.

1.4   Some thoughts for what lies ahead

The worst thing to do when faced with the realisation that you are approaching, or are already in midlife, is to rush into a quick fix based on a superficial understanding of your situation. Moreover, your situation is different from anyone else's and, as you are in the best position to understand it, we will work on this together. Do *not* resign from your job or sell your house; do *not* abandon your family or your friends. It took many years to get to this point. A well-considered delay of a few weeks or a few months while working through this book won't make any difference. Bridges, once torn down, are difficult to rebuild.

The tips and exercises in this book are simple. You do not need to make use of the services of a psychologist, a life coach or a trainer; but you may if you want to.

There are a number of simple, practical activities in this book to assist you. They have been carefully crafted to slowly change the wiring in your brain so that you are mentally able to embrace the new you. There is no other way; you just have to 'put in the hard yards!' Keep all your notes, activities, perceptions and journaling.

They will provide valuable insights in later years. They will be a precious record of your personal growth.

1.5 An overview of your journey

Let's start with an overview of what we are going to do together. We might as well get comfortable with each other now, as we are going to be dealing with some tough issues. Best be prepared for what lies ahead.

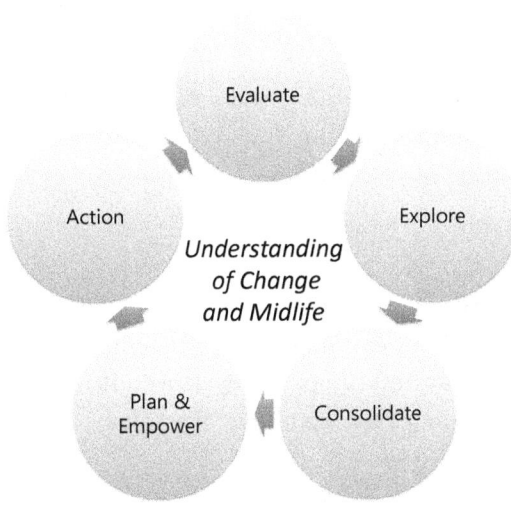

The diagram alongside will help to navigate through the process.

Together we will start by creating a shared understanding of **change** and its effect on us, the role of our **brain** in embracing change, as well as expanding our appreciation of **midlife**.

Thereafter we **evaluate** your life up till now, **explore** a range of opportunities, and **consolidate** these into a package that is right for you. Then we **plan** your process of midlife renewal and **empower** you to take the first steps with confidence and dignity. After that, you take **action** and implement your personal plan with all the celebration and disappointment that will inevitably entail. As you see, it is a circular process, and you may find that you re-cycle through it as you explore and refine your choices and actions. At the end there are some resources to **support** you once you have gone through the open door.

1.6 A quick summary

1. Change

You are about to begin a major life change, and you had better have some concepts and techniques under your belt. You probably have your own views and ideas on change. Change, here, is introduced using a specific view, based on sound concepts, so that we have a common understanding and common vocabulary. It avoids confusion!

2. Brain

Your brain controls your feelings, emotions and actions. It has got used to your current life. You have to help your brain restructure itself to embrace the changes you will make.

3. Midlife

What midlife is and how it can present the opportunity for great personal growth is explored. Don't confuse this with midlife crisis. Midlife is a particular phase of the human life cycle and it is helpful to understand its characteristics and peculiarities.

4. Evaluation

A thoughtful evaluation of your life thus far considers:

- What you have done
- What you have achieved
- What mark you have made on the world.

Let's face it – you have done a great deal in your life. By the time you get to midlife, you have had some spectacular disasters and some spectacular successes. Focus on the achievements. Your achievements, as you understand them, on your terms. Not your mother's view, Uncle George's, or your schoolteacher's. There is something of great value here. Understand your achievements and celebrate them. You have done alright! Recognise that.

5. *Exploration*

Here we discuss which life strategies have worked for you, and which have not. The emphasis is again on your successes and your strengths.

This assessment activity explores the building blocks we will use. Together we are going to build on your strengths. Your strengths are already in place. Your strengths are what you do well; they are what define your role in life. With those insights in place, we will begin exploring options, ideas and new starts. This is the exciting stuff. You will find that you have much more to offer than you realise. In some cases, you might want to make big changes. In other cases, you might just want to revel in the satisfaction of a life well lived and make only a few minor changes.

6. *Consolidation*

Then it is time to arrange all our learnings, through a coherent process, into one consolidated package. What does this mean? What changes do you need to make? Do you need to make any changes at all? You will have to make decisions – on your own and with your loved ones. You may have to abandon old dreams, dreams no longer relevant to your life. These can hold you back, but you will create new ones. This is a difficult time. It is also a time that can be a source of great energy and excitement.

7. *Action*

Then we craft your personal action plan.

- What exactly are you going to do?
- Who is going to participate with you in this adventure?
- When is your completion date?
- What resources do you need?

8. Support

Some helpful ideas on resilience, borrowed from the excellent work of my good friend, Rod Warner, will provide additional support. You will need resilience on your new adventure!

The book concludes with a short list of resources to further assist you.

9. How to get the most out of this book

You will notice that there are quite a few activities in this book. They have been designed with the specific purpose of helping you to fully analyse and assess how you manage your own midlife renewal. Initially you will find them quite difficult because you are revisiting parts of your life you may have forgotten or suppressed. The exercises will not only assist you in gathering and interpreting information about your life, but they are also part of the process of rewiring your brain (see Chapter 3 by Sam Mphuthi on neuro-plasticity). Doing the exercises systematically will greatly improve the value you take from the initiative. You will notice how your awareness of your life situation changes. This is part of opening up new neural pathways in your brain. This is part of the fun.

You have to put in the effort to create your own tools and records. The more you engage, the greater the value you extract, and your handwritten notes will assist with internalisation.

So let us get to it. There is work to be done!

Take Action Now!

Activity 2 – Make a Journal

It helps to keep a journal while going through this process. Any type of book that works for you will do – from the ubiquitous Moleskine™ to an A4 counter book. Or you could use one of the many apps available. It's best to write things down in a book rather than on loose sheets of paper which can easily be mislaid. You will want to come back to your journal and reflect upon your insights. Find a time every day to capture your thoughts and state of mind. Keep it handy and jot down insights as they occur. Describe your emotions. Writing these things down by hand seems to be more effective than capturing them digitally. Even for people like me who have terrible handwriting!

Now, let's go find that open door and unlock it!

Chapter 2

Change

We cannot change anything until we accept it.
— Carl Jung

You are the star performer in the change process that is your midlife career and personal renewal. We are uncomfortable with change because it means that we have to give up certainty and control, and exchange it for the unknown. This is why many of us resist and oppose change.

2.1 Understanding change

This chapter shares a set of concepts to identify and understand your own reactions and the reactions of significant others as you embark on the next phase of your life.

The late William Bridges[1], a great human being and a master of sensitively managing human change in people and organisations, developed the change and transition model we use. I had the opportunity of attending some of his courses in the US and I use his change processes and techniques regularly with my clients. They work for me, they have been of great benefit to my clients, and I am positive that they will work for you. William Bridges created *The Transition Model*, published in his 1991 book *Managing Transitions*.[2]

The model will help you understand your personal, internal transition, and not just the external change going on around you. The difference between 'change' and 'transition' is subtle but important. Change is something that happens to people, even if they don't agree with it. Transition, on the other hand, is internal: it is what happens in people's minds as they go through change. Change can happen very quickly, while transition usually occurs more slowly. We all know people who have actively resisted change. The external change has taken place but they have not made the internal transition.

There are three stages of transition that we go through when we experience change. These are:

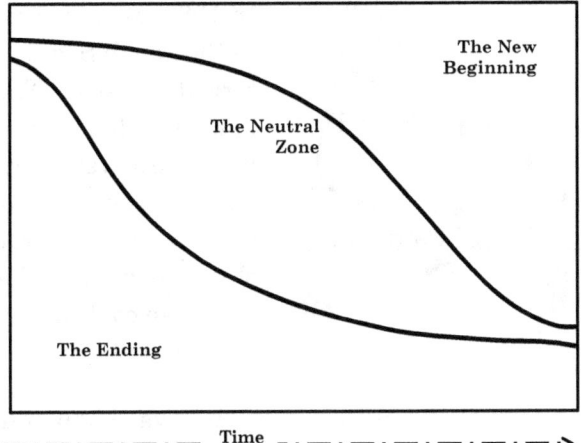

1. *Ending, losing and letting go:* Characterised by resistance and emotional upheaval.

2. *The Neutral Zone:* A period of confusion.

3. *The New Beginning:* Acceptance of the start of a new adventure.

The diagram above shows the uneven way in which the Endings give way to the Neutral Zone and the Neutral Zone to the New Beginnings. More about this later.

Each of us goes through each of the stages of transition at our own pace. It cannot be rushed or slowed down. For example, those who are comfortable with the change will likely move ahead quickly to stage three, while others will linger at stages one or two.

Before examining the transition process in detail, I want to share the 'burning platform' concept with you, introduced to me by Daryl Conner[3] who I met while working for a large corporate. This is a shortened version with a few fictional embellishments to suit our current purpose!

Midlife Renewal: Unlock the Hidden Door

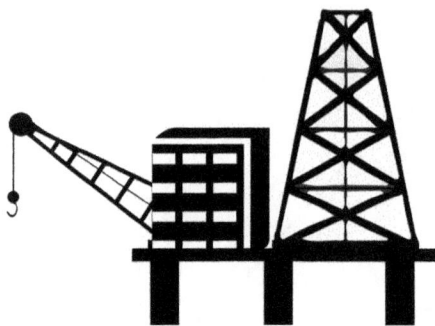

In 1988, an oil rig exploded in the North Sea. It was a terrible disaster. The rig flamed with an intensity that hurt one's eyes. Burning oil on the water covered a wide area. Hard, dangerous objects floated on the icy water, so cold that immersion for only 15 minutes would cause death by hypothermia.

An employee on the rig woke up, saw what was happening, and took stock of the situation in seconds. He weighed up his chances against the inferno of burning oil and flotsam below and jumped fifteen storeys into the water.

Think about the implications for a moment.

- Our colleague could have been killed by impact with the fiery flotsam.
- Without speedy rescue he would have died from hypothermia.
- He may have landed in a sticky, flaming bath of burning oil and died a horrendous death.

Feel the utter terror of the man on the burning platform. If he stays where he is, he will surely die. He doesn't know what will happen when he jumps. The thought of colliding with a floating barrel on fire sends a shudder through his body. The thick burning oil will cling to his face and head, smothering him in flames. He has seconds to make a decision. There is no one to help him talk through the options. Let's face it, these odds are not good.

As it turned out, the man jumped, and he was rescued from the water. A while later he was interviewed for television. The reporter asked him why he had jumped off the platform. Here is my fictional reconstruction of the reply:

Chapter 2: Change

"I was faced with the following options: If I stayed on the rig, I would face certain death. If I jumped, I would face probable death. I chose probable death over certain death."

You see, in the first option, death was inevitable. In the second option, death was highly likely, but there was a slim chance of survival. Hence, the person on the burning platform took the second option. The cost of remaining on the burning platform was too great.

He overcame the terrible fear of the unknown.

The burning platform experience, as described above, is extreme. Hopefully, none of us ever has to experience anything remotely similar. It is important to understand the mechanics of what took place there, so let's unpack it and see what we can learn.

You are in a comfortable place. A change comes along and upsets that comfort. As long as the comfort of the status quo outweighs the cost (discomfort or pain) of embracing the change, no transition (acceptance of the change) will occur.

If, however, the cost of remaining with the status quo is greater than embracing the change, transition will result, according to the three phases. 'Cost' means the social, psychological and human cost, in addition to any financial costs.

Let's apply our new concept. There are many examples of burning platforms surrounding you. A burning platform has preceded every change you have made in life:

- Your car breaks down continually. One day it breaks down in heavy traffic on the way to an important meeting. Enough is enough. The next day you secure a loan to buy a new car.
- You hate your job. One day your boss gives you a particularly hard time in a meeting. The following day you resign.

- Your first child is born. Everything changes, forever.

Get the picture? None of the examples above are as dramatic as the burning platform, but there have been many similar situations in your own life. Change is usually precipitated by an event that causes you to take stock, weigh up the cost of the status quo against the cost of the unknown, and initiate changes that help you deal with the precipitating event.

Without a precipitating event, there will be no change. Take the current situation. You are reading this section of this book right now. Something has happened in your life that has resulted in your reading this book. That is a burning platform. You have a choice ahead of you. To jump or not to jump. Get in touch with the emotions of the man on the platform. Your situation is unlikely to be as intense. Let's help you to make the best choice. Examples of your personal burning platforms are whizzing through your head right now. Hang onto these precipitating events (write them down in your journal) because they will be useful later.

William Bridges has some interesting perspectives on change and transition, explained below.

2.1.1 Stage 1: Ending, losing and letting go

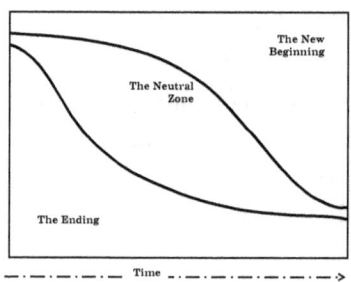

The first stage to master in the change process is the Ending. This is the most difficult stage. Do this well, and the rest will progress more smoothly. This stage begins directly after the burning platform. Still filled with the many emotions of standing on the metaphorical burning platform, you may be angry, confused or just plain irritable. Doubt and confusion grip you. In an extreme case, your world has been turned upside down, and the familiar reference points are gone.

This stage is typically characterised by resistance and emotional upheaval because you are being forced to let go of something familiar and even comfortable. Remember that lovely old car that you would wash and polish on a Saturday afternoon? Your former colleagues, the boss who gave you your first big promotion? The old house? The town you grew up in, with all those memories?

Some, or all, of the following emotions are experienced at this stage:

- *Grief*: There is a sense of loss. Something has to be left behind on that burning platform.
- *Resistance*: You experience a reluctance to move to a new place. It's strange and different.
- *Anger:* You are annoyed because you are losing control over your life as you know it. You are being forced into a situation that is not of your making or of your choice.
- *Sadness*: Something has come to an end. You have to say goodbye.
- *Sense of loss*: The loss of familiar routines, normal situations and material objects leaves a gap in your life.

If you are feeling these or similar emotions, you are in the Endings Zone!

Now here is the important thing. Before beginning to contemplate your renewal, first accept that a phase of your life is ending. By denying the emotions that you are going through, by not acknowledging and accepting them, you are likely to resist the entire change process. When confronted by a big ending, I deal with it by symbolically turning my back on the future and looking backwards into the past. I see what has ended. I ponder over the impact. I absorb the feelings of sadness and loss. I label them and recognise them. I decide what to leave behind. I decide what to take with me. When I am ready, I turn around to face the future and go forward again.

Accept your own resistance and understand your feelings and emotions. Yes, you will resist. Remember that promotion with the big salary increase? A small part of you wanted to stay in the old job because it was comfortable. You had to get used to the new position, the new you. Allow yourself time to accept the change and let go. Continue to support your family, loved ones and colleagues who may be bewildered by your uncharacteristic behaviour.

Successful change and transition management starts not with a bright dream about the future, but with a reflective look at the past and making peace with it, and letting go of people, possessions, aspirations and activities that previously were very important to you. First say "goodbye" to the old you; only then can you say "hello" to the new you. Grasp this, and you have the secret.

Once you understand what it is that you are letting go of, you move on to the Neutral Zone.

2.1.2 Stage 2: The Neutral Zone

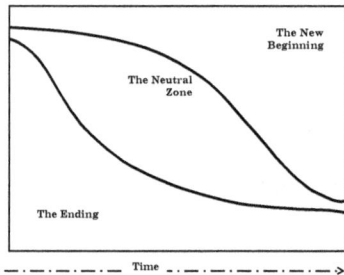

My own experience of the Neutral Zone is largely one of frustration. I knew what I was moving away from, but what I was moving towards was very unclear.

The range of feelings experienced in the Neutral Zone includes:

- Resentment towards the change initiative – look at what I have given up!

- Low morale and low productivity – who cares, whatever! Why bother?

- Anxiety about your emerging role, status or identity – who am I now?

- Scepticism about whether the change will have value for you – will it ever work?

The Neutral Zone is a good time to try things out, experiment with new behaviours and challenge long-held concepts about yourself. Paradoxically, it is a time to take things a bit easier. Ease up. Lighten the diary. Let a few things slip through the cracks.

For men, the role change can be particularly difficult especially if they have lost jobs, changed jobs, or retired. They no longer have the job title or the benefit of a big company 'halo' behind them. They miss the authority of their previous role. If you catch yourself saying "When I was X Manager of Y Company, I did …", realise you are no longer that person. You are becoming someone else.

Despite these difficulties related to role change, this stage can also be one of great creativity, innovation and renewal. This is the perfect time to try new ways of thinking or working.

Your personal challenge during this phase is that you may think that you are unproductive and therefore making little progress. In all likelihood, you will feel lost, without a strong sense of direction. This can persist for quite a while – a few weeks, or even a few months! This is natural and necessary.

Do not get impatient with yourself or try to rush through to stage three. Instead, progress positively and sensitively through the change process. Try to enjoy it! Be gentle with yourself.

Then, one day, you will find yourself ready for the next stage. It happens quite suddenly. It dawns on you: "I am ready to move on." It just happens. You feel it in your bones!

We have all grieved the passing of a loved one. Then we reach a point where we know the period of intense grief is over, even though the memory is with us forever. The same applies here. You will know when it is time to move on.

2.1.3 Stage 3: The New Beginning

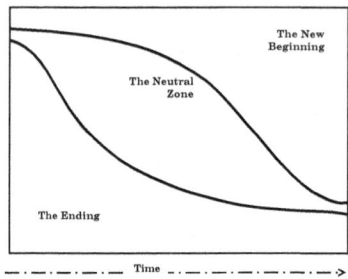

The New Beginning is a time of acceptance and energy. You begin to embrace the new you. While building the skills and insights you need to live successfully in the new way, you start seeing successes.

This is the good time. You may experience:

- High energy levels
- Openness to learning new things and learning about yourself
- Renewed commitment to your redefined role.

Now is the time to celebrate the new you. Be on your guard so that you don't slip back into the old ways; that you don't clamber back on board the burning platform because it is comfortable and familiar.

The diagram below provides a visual illustration. Let's discuss the dynamics:

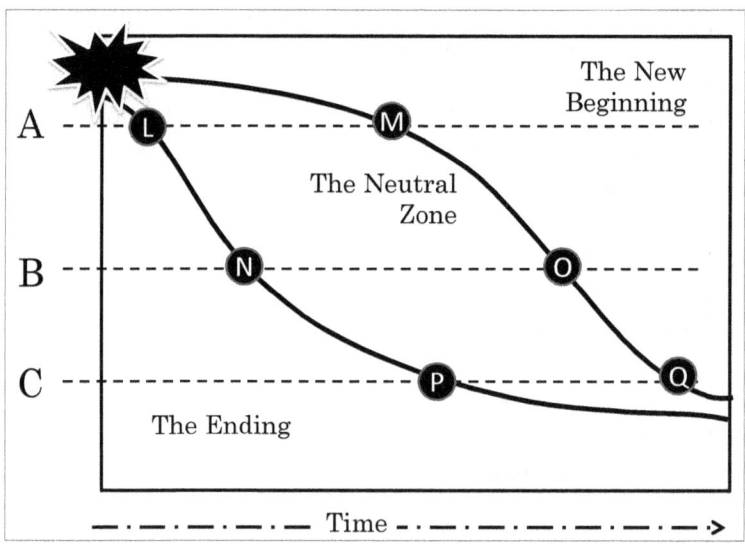

The horizontal axis is time. The flash in the upper left-hand corner is the precipitating event.

Person A responds quickly and gets through the Ending, the Neutral Zone and the New Beginning with ease (A-L-M). Person B takes longer, and spends much more time coming to terms with the Ending and trying to get into the Neutral Zone (B-N-O).

Person C takes even longer. Person C is much more resistant to change, and only comes to terms with what has ended after Person A has made it through to the New Beginnings (C-P-Q).

Why is this important? Certain people may have come to terms with their personal midlife renewal process. They may have decided what changes to make. But a spouse, life partner or colleague may not have the same motivation, and perhaps may be walking the same path to the same conclusions more slowly. It will take him or her much longer to assimilate and respond to the changes that you are proposing.

This is one of the reasons to hesitate before going through the Open Door. Don't leave significant others behind just because they may not have had time to come to terms with your proposals. Also, your significant other might not want to go through that particular Open Door with you. Deciding to proceed on your own and leaving a significant other behind opens a Pandora's box. A whole new cycle of Endings, Neutral Zone and New Beginnings comes into play. Sensitivity and understanding are required to prevent the destruction of important relationships.

Each person is different. Each goes at a different pace. It's important not to rush your progress, nor to drag it out unnecessarily.

The increased energy of New Beginnings facilitates the changes you wish to implement. Psychologically, you are in a positive place, orientated towards your future. The baggage of the past is left there – in the past.

This new perspective and terminology help in understanding what is going on in and around you. The mechanisms and the stages have been explained. You have all you need to take the next step forward.

2.2 Summary

A re-cap of the change and transition sequence and process:

- The *precipitating event/burning platform* happens and a decision must be made to stay with the status quo or move to an unknown new.
- The *Ending* is the period in which we come to terms with what has changed.
- The *Neutral Zone* is a time of confusion when we know the change has happened, but can't quite make out where we are going.
- The *New Beginning* is a phase in which it all makes sense and we can wholeheartedly embrace the new situation.

Now to find out more about how your brain will help you though midlife.

Chapter 3

Your Brain and Midlife

And now at midlife, when the dictates of our souls make themselves known more fully than before, we wake up to discover that our brains and bodies are being re-tooled to facilitate this beautifully.
Christiane Northrup

> *This chapter has been contributed by my good friend and colleague, Sam Mphuthi. Sam is a management consultant and advisor to various national and international organisations and a registered (chartered) clinical psychologist born in the Free State in South Africa. He was educated and employed in various professional positions in Botswana, Zimbabwe, Switzerland and the United Kingdom before returning to South Africa in 1993.*
>
> *Sam and his family live between Johannesburg and Durban, and he consults for public and private sector clients whilst increasingly focusing on writing. He is the author of* Zebras Never Die, *and* Run/Walk for Serenity. *His upcoming titles include:* The Shackled Republic – A perspective on the self-destructive path of South Africa *and* The African in the Black – A view on entrepreneurship ethics, based on African values.
>
> *Over to Sam ...*

3.1 Introduction

In this chapter I am going to share some insights about how your brain works and give you practical insights into how you can rewire your brain to get the best out of your renewal adventure.

We are going to start with a high-level overview of the brain and the part it plays in shaping our experience of and our responses to how we think, how we feel and how we behave. This is a very complex area, and we are going to summarise it to give you the key understandings to enable you to respond positively to your own renewal. We will also banish any thoughts that the brain loses functionality and atrophies with age. Quite the opposite, in fact. A healthy brain is a critical part of a fulfilling second half.

We are not going to deal with pathological conditions and dysfunctional states, nor therapies associated with assisting individuals regain quality of life following pathology or dysfunction. These are very important areas of human experience but cannot be treated in a book of this nature. Where there is a need or specific interest in these issues, we recommend that a clinical psychologist with a specialisation in neuropsychology or a psychiatrist be consulted for advice.

In the preceding chapters you will have discovered that renewal involves thoughts, feelings and actions (behaviour) that combine in particular ways to result in new ways of conducting and experiencing your life.

We might not have thought about it, but everyone shares an understanding that our thoughts, our feelings and our behaviours are perceived, modulated and acted upon by the brain. The brain is the command centre that interprets these inputs and helps us respond to our inner and outer world. So if we are going to make the most of our midlife renewal, we should understand how this inner command centre works, because you are going to re-programme it to do different things for you.

We are now going to discuss the following:

- A high-level view of brain functions relevant to renewal
- A broad description of how the brain works
- A view on how the brain changes and supports changes that come with renewal.

The brain oversees three functions:

- **Emotions** – it regulates how we respond to threats or rewards; fear, pleasure
- **Thinking** – memorising, planning and focusing
- **Self-regulation** of these functions.

Most people are able to self-regulate their emotions, thoughts and feelings most of the time. The process of midlife renewal is bound to bring out strong emotions, different or more intense forms of thinking, or strong physiological reactions to an event or to our own thoughts and feelings. It is how the brain accommodates to the new situation that determines a successful renewal. In the same way that an understanding of change helps us to deal with our own renewal process, we have to understand how our brain responds to renewal, so that we can use it as a source of positive personal growth.

Let's take a simplified high-level overview of the brain. You probably know most of this, but let's put it together in the context of your personal renewal process.

3.2 Simplified anatomy of the brain and functions

The brain consists of the cerebral cortex and is divided into two parts or hemispheres. Linking the two is an information superhighway called the corpus callosum. The corpus callosum enables communication between the two hemispheres of the brain. It is like a switchboard that is responsible for transmitting neural messages between the right and left hemispheres. The communication between the two hemispheres enables the brain to perform sophisticated tasks that cause processes originating in the opposite hemispheres to combine in order to achieve specific outcomes. For instance, you are able to use your hands and eyes to gently build a house of playing cards in a coordinated manner because there is harmonisation between the hemispheres.

3.2.1 Central communications

Certain functions tend to reside in one hemisphere and others in the other. But this is by no means cut and dried. There are no brain functions that take place exclusively in one section of a hemisphere. Combination of functions across the hemispheres also takes place at higher mental function level, referred to as 'cognitive' synthesis. An example is the coordination of visual images that initially originate separately in the hemispheres. The 'interpretation' of the image subsequently seen by the combined processing of the left and right eyes is possible because there is communication between the spheres, resulting in the brain performing cognitive 'integration' or 'synthesis'. The outcome in this case is one where the individual attributes higher-level meaning to the image than would be the case without the integration between the hemispheres. For instance, you may interpret what you have seen as desirable, beautiful, threatening, uneventful, and so on, as a result of the brain performing a sophisticated combination of the domains across the hemispheres. The thoughts and/or feelings that you attribute to the visual experience will lead you to act in a manner deemed appropriate according to your interpretation of the experience.

There are other regions of the brain, but they are not relevant to our central theme.

3.2.2 Brain cells

Now let's consider the building blocks of your brain

Neurons

The brain is made up of a very large number of brain cells called neurons. The electrical activity between the neurons makes brain functioning possible. Connectivity or communication between the hemispheres as well as between and within regions of the brain takes place through the electrical activity of the brain cell or neuron. This electrical activity consists of bits of information moving about inside our brain.

Over time, they tend to settle down to regular and predictable pathways. Neurons are specialised cells designed to transmit information to other nerve cells, muscle or gland cells. The neuron receives, processes and transmits information through electrical and chemical signals. These signals between neurons occur via specialised connections called synapses.

Typically, a neuron has the following parts: a cell body that directs all activities of the neuron; dendrites (the part that looks like tree branches), which are short fibres that receive messages from other neurons and relay those messages to the cell body; and the axon, a long, single fibre that transmits electrical impulses to the next adjacent cell.

Neurons are stimulated to initiate nerve impulses. The generation of a nerve impulse requires ADEQUATE stimulus. Unlike the motor neurons of muscle contraction, brain neurons can be either stimulated or inhibited. In other words, they can be made to do something or they can be made not to do something.

A neuron can receive stimulatory and inhibitory signals at the same time. If the neuron doesn't receive adequate stimulus, it can't produce a nerve impulse.

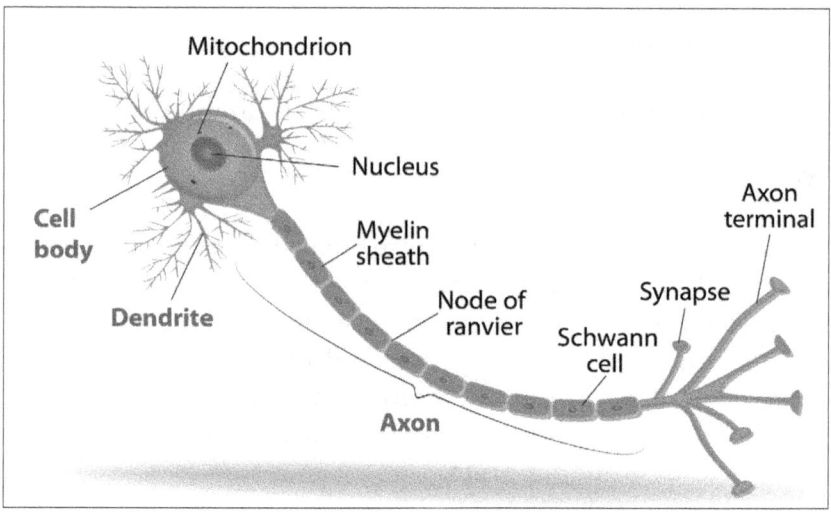

Figure 1: A typical neuron[4]

Neural networks

A biological neural network is a series of interconnected neurons whose activation defines a recognisable linear pathway. The interface through which neurons interact with their neighbours usually consists of several axon terminals connected via synapses to dendrites on other neurons.

How neural networks are formed

The connections between neurons are called synapses – they typically link the axon of a neuron with the cell body or a dendrite of another neuron. Think of them as a series of electrical extension leads plugged together.

Synaptic plasticity involves the strengthening and weakening of synapses. Some pathways may be more favoured, and others less favoured. This happens over time, as we become settled and consistent in our job, our family and our circle of friends. They settle down into comfortable, efficient circuits. And it is the re-casting of these pathways, or circuits, that are important for midlife renewal, allowing us to create new pathways, alternative pathways and adapting old pathways.

3.2.3 Regions of the brain and connectivity between the regions

The brain has two hemispheres with specialised functions or domains but the hemispheres communicate with each other to result in the outcomes that we experience as thought, feelings and behaviour. They work together as a team.

Think of it like this: each hemisphere is a province; the corpus callosum is the suspension bridge between the two provinces. Each hemisphere has lots of towns. And in each town are many suburbs, streets and open areas.

Information highways, streets and lanes

Just as there is communication between the hemispheres of the brain, there is communication between the areas of the brain within the hemispheres.

For our purposes, we focus on connectivity across the different brain areas of the neocortex. This is a gross over-simplification, but we want to create a broad understanding of how we are able to 'rewire' our brains when we embark on our renewal venture. In fact, if we want to be successful in our renewal, we have no choice but to rewire our brains.

What can go wrong, go wrong, go wrong ... (hyper- and hypocoherence)

When coherence is in balance, all is well. But sometimes it goes out of balance. There are two forms of dysfunctional coherence. Hypercoherence takes place when there is too much sharing. Hypocoherence takes place when too little sharing occurs.

When you look at an object, the areas in your brain responsible for visual processing usually respond with relevant activity so that you can identify an object along with its size, shape and colour. Hypercoherence happens when several areas of the brain that have different 'specialisations' respond to a stimulus (an object, process, or event) at the same time, thus slowing information processing. In other words, when other areas of your brain that are not specialised in visual processing are stimulated (i.e. 'attempting' to process a visual stimulus), it interferes with (slows down) the processes of the areas specialised in visual processing. Thus, there is 'too much sharing' between areas that are supposed to perform specialised functions, resulting in inefficient (slower than normal) information processing. A person with hypercoherence will look at an object and parts of the brain unconnected with visual processing will light up. This additional workload will slow down the process of visual recognition, and it will take the person longer to identify the shape, colour and size of an object.

Think of someone learning to play the clarinet. You have to read the music, do the finger work, hit the right notes and hold the tune. The early learning stages are completely overwhelming for a learner who has never learnt music or the clarinet.

Hypocoherence, on the other hand, occurs when there is no sharing between areas relevant for the stimulus e.g. if the visual processing areas do not connect or are connecting incorrectly to the verbal processing (language, coding) areas of the brain, then the object seen by the visual processing areas is not fully identified. Thus you might not be able to label the object as 'big', 'bright', or 'small' because the verbal area has not received (or connected correctly) with the visual area. This 'disconnection' is aptly termed hypocoherence i.e. the lack of coherence. A person with hypocoherence will look at an object and will not be able to recognise it. The connections to identify the shape, colour and size of an object will not take place.

Our learner clarinet player may look at the sheet music, look at the holes on the clarinet and be completely overwhelmed. She does not know how to respond.

The good news is that dysfunctional hyper- and hypocoherence affect very few people. But understanding coherence will provide deeper insights into your renewal rewiring.

Phase lag

Closely linked to coherence is 'phase lag'. Phase lag describes the speed of communication between two locations. If communication between different parts of the brain takes place too fast, inhibitory mechanisms cannot intervene. If communication between different parts of the brain takes place too slowly, this will result in slow cortical processing.

Decreased phase lag means there is 'decreased time' in sharing i.e. the sharing is taking place too fast. This means the individual will not have adequate time to 'inhibit' inappropriate thoughts, feelings or behaviour.

Conversely, increased phase lag means that there is an 'increase' in the time ('too long') taken to share the information between specialised areas. This results in inefficient processing of the information.

Let's illustrate this with two examples.

Decreased phase lag	Increased phase lag
A person with decreased phase lag sees someone wearing an ugly jersey. She blurts out: "What and ugly jersey!" without taking account of the feelings of the person who is wearing the jersey.	A person with increased phase lag will see someone about to tip a pot of boiling water over them and will not react in time to prevent the accident.

During renewal, especially during the 'Neutral Zone', what is experienced as 'confusion' or lack of clarity, very often is due to very minor coherence and phase lag problems. Your brain has to consider options and scenarios that it has never had to contemplate before.

Symptoms of this include:

- You feel overwhelmed.
- You have difficulty in discriminating between different options confronting you.
- You struggle to evaluate the implications of a course of action.
- You struggle to get things done.
- You find yourself daydreaming.

When you recognise these symptoms in your personal renewal journey you have affirming evidence that you are gradually rewiring your brain to take you into the next exciting phase of your life. As you come to grips with your new situation, your brain progressively, step by step, achieves new coherence and phase lag calibration when processing new thoughts, feelings and behaviour. These brain connectivity activities set in motion neuroplasticity at brain cell level. The discomfort you experience is not dysfunctional. You should not be alarmed. Your brain is just 2% of your body mass, but it uses 20% of your body's available energy. You are creating new sets of pathways in your brain. I like to think of it as a bulldozer in your brain, levelling out new roadways. It's hard work and lots of power is involved! During renewal you are rebuilding and redirecting the information highways in your brain.

3.3 Physically changing the brain through learning and renewal (change)

This is where it gets interesting!

Here are two definitions of plasticity:[5]

1. the quality or state of being plastic; especially: capacity for being moulded or altered
2. the capacity for continuous alteration of the neural pathways and synapses of the living brain and nervous system **in response to experience or injury**.

Neuroplasticity incorporates the notion of being able to reshape and rework the brain. It also encompasses the reshaping of your neural pathways in response to new experiences (or the affirming prospect of future experiences!).

3.3.1 Overview of change in the brain and relevance for renewal

We have now discovered that neuroplasticity is the ability of the brain to change and reorganise itself by forming new neural circuits. This takes place throughout our lives. The adult brain is much more capable of physical and chemical change than is generally thought. Neuroplasticity allows the nerve cells in the brain to adjust their activities in response to new situations or to changes in their environment. Neuroplasticity was initially discovered in trying to understand how neurons enable the brain to compensate following injury to regions of the brain that usually carry out those functions.

Neuroplasticity involves 'reconfiguring' or 'rewiring' of the brain by creating new connections (pathways or circuitry) between neurons that results in a 'reshaped' brain anatomy and functioning. Simply put, when one part of the brain cannot function properly, another part of the brain compensates. Thus, the brain's architecture continues to change throughout adulthood, and this can be manipulated for enhanced capacity and functioning where individuals are exploring new experiences or new environments. In this regard, neuroplasticity can simply be a 'collaboration' between neurons for increased efficiency in processing information or experiences.

Repetition and the brain

This means that when people repeatedly practise an activity or access a memory, their neural networks – groups of neurons that fire together, creating electrochemical pathways – shape themselves according to that activity or memory. When people stop practising new things, the brain will eventually eliminate, or 'prune', the connecting cells that formed the pathways. Like in a system of freeways connecting various cities, the more cars going to a certain destination, the wider the road that carries them needs to be. The fewer cars travelling that way, however, the fewer lanes are needed.

"If you perform a task or recall some information that causes different neurons to fire in concert, it strengthens the connections between those cells. Over time, these connections become thick, hardy road maps that link various parts of the brain – and stimulating one neuron in the sequence is more likely to trigger the next one to fire. The more times the network is stimulated, the stronger and more efficient it becomes."[6]

Neurons in a network that fire at the same time create a bond that enables them to connect more strongly. This happens over time. As the connections entrench themselves, fewer neurons are required to perform the task. If the firing is related to a physical task or a cognitive process, the firing of the circuits combines to produce greater efficiency through reception. The neurons become faster and more efficient, requiring fewer to keep the skill functioning. This is what happens when mastering a technique such as playing the piano. Concert pianists owe a large part of their brilliance not just to their genetic inheritance, but because they have practised and practised and in so doing have built up the efficient pathways to make this skill seem effortless.

This is more efficient for performing the task at hand, but this means that other networks or brain areas are not enhanced.

3.3.2 The impact of new experiences

New experiences such as learning a new language or learning to play a musical instrument lead to physical changes of the brain. New circuits awaken, leading to different pathways lighting up across the brain. Thus, the process of personal renewal is able to 'rewire' the brain. The brain is remarkably plastic. Even in middle or old age, it's still adapting very actively to its environment. This is an exciting insight for you in your personal process of renewal.

Our brain continues to create new neurons throughout our lives. Neuroplasticity has tremendous consequences. It means that, whoever we are, whatever we've become, it is always possible to change. Change and embracing new ideas and new skills is good for your brain. Renewal is essential for your continued health and wellbeing in the second half of your life.

3.4 Linking one's brain functioning to renewal

When individuals go through a process of profound personal renewal, a whole new set of pathways are chained together in the brain.

3.4.1 **The Endings supported by interhemispheric synthesis and integration**

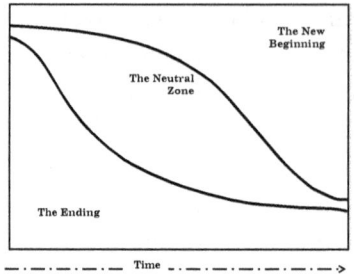

You will recall our Endings, Neutral zone, New Beginnings diagram in the previous chapter.

A burning platform makes you consider new ways of responding to a life situation. This is why it is so difficult to embrace the change. Your brain has been wired for a certain set of circumstances, and now those circumstances have changed. You are dealing with a range of new and different thoughts, emotions and feelings. This is why the thoughts, feelings and actions you experience at this time are so volatile. You are forced to begin the process of rewiring. This is what is involved when embracing the burning platform.

This is one of the reasons why the Endings is such an awkward period. You have to utilise different parts of your brain, at all levels, in order to process the changes that are confronting you. Those parts of the brain have not yet developed the pathways for efficiency.

3.4.2 **The Neutral Zone supported by cerebral specialisation and neural networks**

The Neutral Zone is a time of frustration. You know what you are moving away from, but what you are moving towards is very unclear. The Neutral Zone is a good time to try things out, experiment with new behaviours and challenge long-held concepts of yourself.

One of the reasons why the Neutral Zone is a confusing and bewildering period is because you are undertaking the process of rewiring. You are considering options, learning new skills, understanding this differently. Your brain is in the midst of a massive rewiring. You are beginning to test your new reality as the process of neuroplasticity restructuring takes place

New competencies are gained with new neural networks, resulting in new experiences of thoughts, feelings and behaviours. Your rewiring has restructured when you realise are ready to move on with your life.

3.4.3 The New Beginnings reinforced by attained neuroplasticity

Once you have come to terms with your renewed reality, once the rewiring takes place, you are in a position to undertake the New Beginning.

The New Beginning is a time of acceptance and energy. Your brain has achieved new efficiencies in the rewiring process. You will have begun to embrace the new you. You will be building the skills and insights you need to live successfully in the new way, and you will start seeing successes. This is the good time. You will experience higher energy levels, you will be open to learning new things and learning about yourself, and you will have mapped out your redefined role. Your brain will have reconfigured to the new situation.

At cell level, the brain cells (neurons) have formed new connections to support your ongoing ability to function effectively and efficiently in the new-found competencies/experiences.

You, quite literally, have renewed yourself. You have a new upgraded brain!

In support of this, James and I have developed the Forson-Mphuthi Model of Neurocognitive Renewal Restructuring:

Renewal	Brain processes
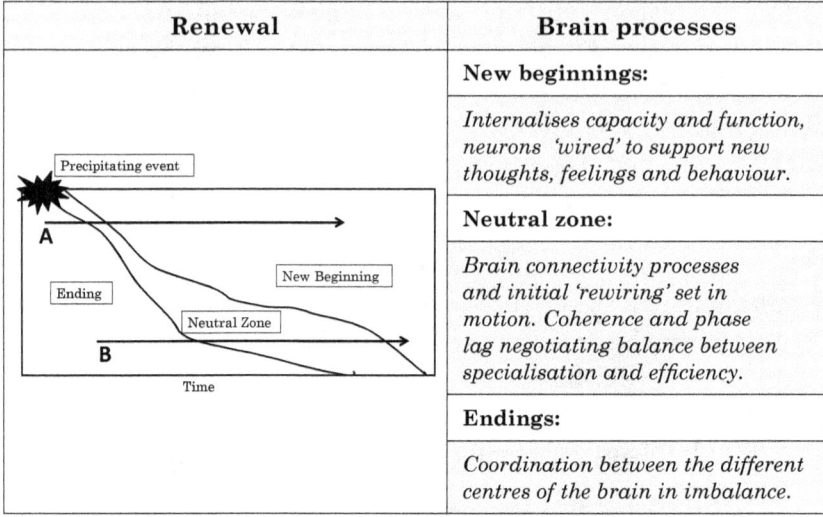	**New beginnings:**
	Internalises capacity and function, neurons 'wired' to support new thoughts, feelings and behaviour.
	Neutral zone:
	Brain connectivity processes and initial 'rewiring' set in motion. Coherence and phase lag negotiating balance between specialisation and efficiency.
	Endings:
	Coordination between the different centres of the brain in imbalance.

Figure 2: The Forson-Mphuthi Neurocognitive Renewal Model

Your brain hemispheres collaborate to address the challenges of renewal. This is the challenge of dealing with Endings. The rewiring process is set in motion to find new calibration for coherence and phase lag. This occurs during the Neutral Zone. The rewired brain supports the new thoughts, feelings and behaviour once you have progressed to the New Beginnings. Now you have a practical framework for understanding the mechanics of change and your personal response and adaptation to change!

3.4.4 Brain health

Your brain is a wonderful complex part of who you are. To enjoy the fruits of your renewal you need to keep it healthy. The following habits will ensure that your brain continues to perform its critical role:

- **Get enough sleep.** Sleep is poorly understood but enough sleep is essential for a healthy brain. Better brain and physical health in older people is related to getting an average of seven to eight hours of sleep every 24 hours. It's a myth that adults need less sleep as they age. Chronic inadequate sleep puts people at higher risk for dementia, depression, heart disease, obesity, diabetes, fall-related injuries and cancer.

- **Eat healthily.** Fresh nourishing food keeps your brain in peak condition. Fresh fruits, vegetables, fish and nuts will protect your brain, fight fatigue, ward off aging, and boost your mood and alertness.

- **Drink sufficient water.** Water hydrates us and flushes impurities away. It is important to drink water throughout the day for optimal brain function because your brain does not have any way to store water. When your body loses more water than you are replacing, dehydration kicks in and your brain function will be affected.

- **Get enough exercise.** Regular exercise promotes a sense of well-being and has beneficial advantages for your brain. Exercise helps to reduce insulin resistance, reduce inflammation, and stimulate the release of growth factors – chemicals in the brain that affect the health of brain cells, the growth of new blood vessels in the brain, and even the abundance and survival of new brain cells. Exercise improves mood and sleep, and reduces stress and anxiety. Problems in these areas frequently cause or contribute to cognitive impairment.

- **Maintain healthy social relationships.** We are social beings. Just as human beings have a basic need for food and shelter, we also have a basic need to belong to a group and form relationships. The desire to be in a loving relationship, to fit in with a group, to avoid rejection and loss, to see your friends do well and be cared for, to share good news with your family – these things motivate an incredibly impressive array of our thoughts, actions and feelings, and as we know, thoughts, actions and feelings are part of how our brain works.

- **Keep on learning new things.** Learning is rewiring. The more we do it, the healthier our brains are. We can change the structure of our brains and increase our capacity to learn.

If the brain is not challenged with new learning, its function can gradually erode over time, leading to decreased memory and cognitive function.

- **Avoid prolonged negative stress.** Stress can sap your resolve and break down your resilience. You can do something about it. Chronic stress – continual stress – results in increased cortisol production. Cortisol creates a surplus of the neurotransmitter glutamate. Glutamate creates free radicals – unattached oxygen molecules – that attack brain cells causing decay. Stress can also:
  - make you forgetful and emotional.
  - create a vicious cycle of fear and anxiety.
  - deplete critical brain chemicals causing depression.
  - put you at greater risk for mental illnesses of all kinds, including depression, dementia and Alzheimer's.

So, look after your brain – it's the only one you have!

3.5 Conclusion

The brain physically changes every time it learns something. And there are ways to keep that happening. Intelligence is not fixed, it turns out, nor planted firmly in our brains from birth. Rather, it's forming and developing throughout our lives. The better you get at managing your brain's rewiring, the healthier your brain will be. As we mentioned in the opening paragraph of this chapter, your brain is the command centre that interprets and helps you to respond to your inner and outer world. Make your brain more efficient and many positive benefits result for your thoughts, your feelings and your behaviours.

Learning is the formation of new or stronger neural connections. To improve our brain functioning it helps to prioritise activities that help us build on already-existing pathways (for instance, by integrating work activities relevant to life experience). For example, if you are a bookkeeper and you become treasurer of a scuba diving club, you will fit into the scuba diving enterprise more rapidly than if there is no link to your current life experience.

Whenever new material is processed with involvement of known relationships, you generate greater brain cell activity and achieve more successful long-term memory storage and retrieval related to the new material or activity.

We need to break through those neuro-mythological barriers that tell us that intelligence and aptitude are set at birth and cannot be changed. This is particularly important when we may have believed that we cannot do something because we are 'not smart', or 'we can't draw', or 'we will never be able to write a book'.

Once we realise that we can change our brain through learning and relating new contexts to what is already known, we are on our way to a new, empowered self.

So, in conclusion, your brain is part of your process of renewal. As you decide on the actions you will take, your brain is creating new circuits and pathways to deal with the challenges you are creating for it. That is why it is important to perform the 'Take Action Now' activities in this book. Your brain is plastic, so by learning new skills, embracing new ideas or new activities, your brain will alter to support you in your new endeavours. This means that in the process of renewal, your thoughts, feelings and actions will change to support the new understanding of who you are.

Chapter 4

Midlife

*Life belongs to the living, and he who lives must be
prepared for changes.*
Johann Wolfgang von Goethe

Midlife is a time of change. It can start in the mid-thirties, or any time up to our mid-sixties. It is the time where you, at a deep personal level, realise that there are fewer days ahead of you than behind you. Read that again:

There are fewer days ahead of you than behind you.

Pause, and let the words sink in.

With this comes the realisation that you will not achieve some of your cherished dreams or life goals. It is a very sobering realisation. You confront your own mortality. You realise that your death is not some distant event, but imminent, around the corner – the last adventure. It becomes a tangible inevitability rather than a remote possibility. So it makes sense to put the months, years or decades left in your life to good use.

Many people hurt themselves and those they love by resisting the change that midlife requires, spending too long on the burning platform and frying themselves in the process. Families and yourself are torn apart by holding onto the past during this time of change and transition. Often, the pain of resisting change causes people to go back to their old habits. They become crotchety and angry – the archetype of the grumpy old man, or the embittered old woman! Our insights about the brain give us an advantage here. Far preferable is a successful midlife, a comfortable environment free from pain of any sort.

Facing up to the challenge of reinventing ourselves is vital. Midlife transformation can be one of the most beautiful and amazing times in life when it evolves simultaneously with inner, personal change along with the support and participation of others.

Understand that midlife is not tightly defined. It is not an event. Puberty and menopause are defined by specific physical changes. Midlife has no such defining features. It is what you want it to be, dependent on how you respond to it.

4.1 Time to step back

By the time midlife comes along, a few things have been sorted out. You are no longer an awkward pimply teenager and your career has been developed, as well as significant job and life skills, and expertise in relationships. You know a great deal about life.

Midlife is a good time to consider the following:

- Midlife is a time of mental, physical and spiritual renewal and evolution.
- It can be a time to break out of mismatched relationships.
- You have the maturity to experiment with new perspectives on the world and ways of perceiving yourself.
- You can pause to simplify. You can decide what relationships, possessions and emotional baggage you want to carry forward.
- Midlife renewal is a process that spans years. You can grow into it.

One of the sobering realisations of midlife is that you may have to say goodbye to unfulfilled and cherished dreams of younger days. Becoming an astronaut, for example, but who wants to train a 47-year-old plumber to be an astronaut? You may have wanted to climb Mount Everest, but your body is not even going to get the top of the local hill because you have not invested in the necessary long-term training. You may want to be the CEO of your company, but other more competent or more favoured people are further along the promotion queue. You may want to travel the world, but you do not have the financial resources to do so.

You are not a failure if you haven't achieved all your dreams; look at your other great achievements. Dreams are just that: dreams. You have managed to do some pretty inspiring things in your life. You tend to write off your achievements because you are so familiar with them. In the era of the 'bucket list', we are made to feel that our lives are unfulfilled or incomplete if we have not done a hundred outrageous things.

Not so. Not at all.

The people who compile and pursue bucket lists often do so because they think that climbing a mountain or walking the El Camino de Santiago makes them more acceptable. It enhances their sense of self-worth. I have never known someone who has compiled a bucket list who does not broadcast the details to all and sundry. It is as much, if not more, about the "oohs" and "ahs" of jealous admirers, as the actual accomplishments. They feel their everyday lives are not worthy without this applause. You, on the other hand, as we shall see, are a very worthy person. Applause is wonderful if it happens, but you don't need applause to be special.

4.2 Taking stock

The midlife, then, is a time to take stock of your goals, dreams and opportunities that can still be realised. It is also the time to let go of some of the goals and dreams that cannot, or are not possible to be fulfilled due to resource constraints. Midlife is the time to look back down the corridor of life and evaluate successes and failures. Believe me, we all have magnificent piles of failures, but never allow these to get in the way of achieving successes in the future. Some of us may not be in the best of health. Some of us may have onerous financial commitments to service. Others have family and other obligations that cannot be changed. These are all facts. But you can change how you feel and act in relation to them.

Whatever your situation, whatever your earnings, whatever your skills, the second half of your life can and should be a time of personal growth, a time of understanding, of serenity and personal joy. You cannot readily change your circumstances, but you can change the way you react to them.

Within the process of change resides the loss of old comforts and support. Painful moments often have to be embraced, re-experienced and accepted before the transition runs its course and closure is reached. This is the time of coming to terms with what has ended, what is now consigned to the past.

To start this process you have to accept that your nature is changing. You are becoming a different person. Approach this time of life as one of transformation and opportunity; it is time to address the needs of your mind, body and spirit. Welcome to the second half of your life. You are now a 'second-halfer'.

4.3 Summary

Midlife brings the realisation that you do not have unlimited time. Take action to live a rewarding and fulfilling life – right up to the end. It's not a time of desperation. It's a time of grace and serenity. You have started to take control. Well done!

Activity 3 – Reward Yourself

Reward yourself with a cup of coffee or a walk in the park. Savour the moment. Allow yourself to rejoice a little. The adventure is about to begin!

4.4 Case Study: Richard the banker

Richard was the quintessential banker. Invisible, grey and with a dry sense of humour. He had an encyclopaedic understanding of banking bureaucracy and could play the organisational politics to his advantage. If you wanted to get something done, Richard was your go-to man. He was in his early fifties and lived a sober life, managing his finances very carefully. His path to a comfortable retirement was minutely mapped out.

Then a restructuring came about. Richard, ever meticulous, sat down and carefully considered his situation, making copious notes which he carefully shared with his wife. With unforeseen results:

> *"You know, I realised that I was my own biggest enemy. Here I was with thirty years' experience in the bank. All I had was matric and my bankers' exams. But I had so much experience about people and organisations. I really understood how to work with people. But I was just so darn comfortable. I realised that if I was going to change, I had to do it now."*

So Richard read some books, changed his haircut, swopped his dark suit for a striped shirt and set himself up as a mentor to young managers. Youngsters starting out in their careers liked him because he was not demanding, but got the best out of them. He had a good style. He had always been good about managing money and the family did not have to adjust their lifestyle.

The transformation was obvious. Richard looked twenty years younger and the grey banker persona had disappeared. He seemed alive and full of life.

Then Richard was involved in an accident and this reduced his mobility. He started doing his mentoring work online, but then a new opportunity opened up. He volunteered to be the unpaid au pair and homework supervisor for his grandchildren, and he loves every moment spent with them. He and his wife have joined a walking club, and he is slowly improving his strength.

A midlife renewal has been a wonderful, positive experience for Richard.

Chapter 4: Midlife

 Richard's learnings from this experience:

- You don't need formal qualifications to undertake midlife renewal.
- Face up to the situation and be honest with yourself.
- Take on responsibilities for which you won't be paid.
- Sometimes your physical frailties force you to adjust your expectations.
- Not everything you do has to be for money.

Chapter 5

Evaluation

You can act to change and control your life; and the procedure, the process is its own reward.
— Amelia Earhart

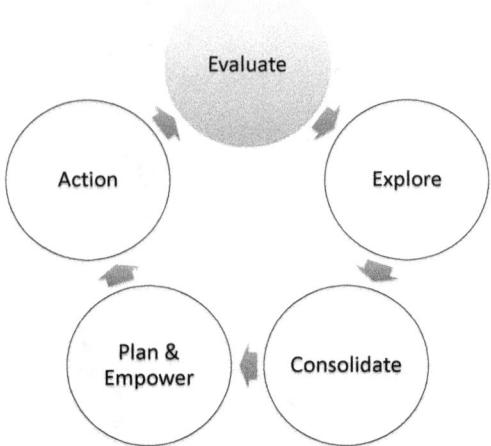

T hus far we have shared some ideas about change and transition, your brain and about midlife. Now to get down to the specifics. Unpacking your life.

Life evaluation is an important step in a midlife review. This is the time to look back at the experiences that have shaped you and those that have left their mark on you.

This is the first step towards renewal. At each stage on the chart below, record your progress to keep track.

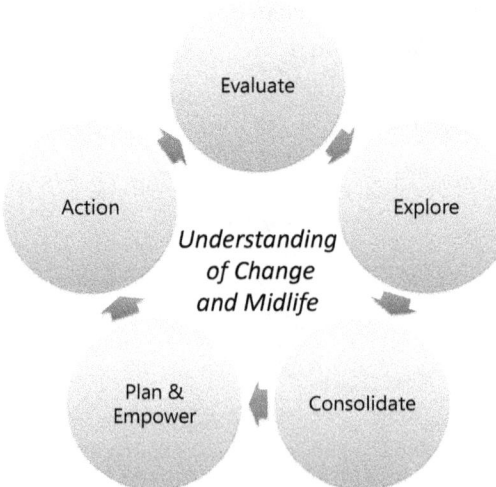

In our early- to mid-20s, we have great dreams, and a great desire for outstanding achievements. Life stretches before us to infinity, with no perceptible end. There is all the time in the world. Then – we become stuck in adulthood. We get lost in the drudgery of day-to-day work, in family relationships and other activities. All are important, and keep us occupied. The days, weeks, months and years go by and suddenly, we are middle-aged.

We all appreciate the quote from Annie Dillard:[7]

"How we spend our days is, of course, how we spend our lives."
Annie Dillard

Everybody has this realisation at some stage or another in their lives; you and I are no different. The challenge facing us is making sure to react positively and assertively. At this point, we are building up to confirming and defining your own personal burning platform.

You can review your life with a number of exercises and techniques. One that I propose is compiling your life timeline. A timeline is extremely useful. It allows you to recognise past trends, locate the watershed events and to pick out critical decision points in your life. There are a number of different approaches to constructing a timeline. (Use your browser to search for other approaches.)

5.1 Creating your own life timeline

A life timeline helps to:

- Identify the times of your life when you were happiest and the times that were not so happy
- Establish the patterns of your life with regard to relationships and jobs
- Track your career evolution
- Track your growth as a human being
- Understand your personal life journey.

Why are we doing this? We second-halfers know we are in the second half of the one-off 'game of life'. There is no half-time break to go to the change room to plan the rest of the game. We have to make it happen here on the field of play. We have to do it right. There are wonderful rewards if we succeed.

- Let's live the rest of our lives to the full, with dignity.
- Let's take the good stuff from the past with us.
- Let's avoid the negative in our lives.
- Let's make sure that in the last half we do the right things – for ourselves and for our loved ones.

5.1.1 Building a timeline

There are different ways of developing a personal timeline. Work out the best way of doing yours – electronic or hard copy, vertical or horizontal. Most people seem to go old-school with pencil and paper. It is not about the presentation, it is about the process. But, you knew that!

An easy way to do this is as follows:

1. Stick sheets of ruled paper together until it resembles a long scroll. Allow two lines per year of life and add space for at least another ten years.
2. Rule a narrow column on the left-hand side and write in each year, starting with your date of birth.
3. Add another column next to the first and capture your age in years.
4. Divide the remaining space in half vertically – one column for events, the other for comments. The comments relate to how you felt – for instance, there may have been a difference between events you chose and those that simply occurred, like family decisions or factors outside your control.
5. I then go down the event column and capture the events that have occurred in my life. I put down anything that was important then, and that which is still important now.

An excerpt from my personal timeline appears on the next page as an example.

Chapter 5: Evaluation

Year	Age	Events	Evaluation
1955	0	I was born in Worcester	
1956	1	We moved to Cape Town	
1957	2		
1958	3		
1959	4	We moved to Johannesburg	I have very little recollection of this.
1960	5	My father died. We moved back to Worcester	My father's death was traumatic. We were left with very little money. My mother and I had to move in with my grandmother in Worcester. My brother stayed with an uncle and aunt.
1961	6	I started school	
1962	7		
1963	8		
1964	9		
1965	10	My brother left school and left town.	This was a difficult time. My mother and her sisters were having a difficult time, and I was distressed because my elder brother was no longer around.
1966	11		
1967	12		
1968	13	Started high school. I moved in with my uncle and aunt	
1969	14		
1970	15	Took rugby seriously	I was never good at rugby, but I always got a game for the third team. It was good for my sense of self worth
1971	16		
1972	17	I finished school	This was a difficult year as my grandmother died midyear and my aunt died just before matric exams.
1973	18	National service in the infantry	It was good to be away from home. But the army was not the place for me. Essentially it was a waste of a year.
1974	19	Registered as a student at UCT	Living and studying in Cape Town was a life changing experience. Open to new ideas and meeting and making new friends.
1975	20		
1976	21		
1977	22	Completed four years, but with no degree	It was disappointing not having a degree but I had not applied myself to my studies
1978	23	Became a plant operator on a diamond mine in the Northern Cape	I saw an advert in a newspaper, applied for it, and got the job
1979	24		The job meant shift work, and it was a very lonely existence
1980	25	Moved to Namibia - training officer with a mining company	This was an exciting development.
1981	26		I achieved a great deal of success under a supportive mentor
1982	27	Returned to UCT to complete Bachelor's degree	I went back to UCT to finish my degree. Being a mature student meant I applied myself much better to study
1983	28	Stayed on for Honours	I stayed on a further year to complete honours. I was doing project work for the mining company in the holidays.
1984	29	Completed an MBA at UCT	It had always been my aspiration to do an MBA, so I stayed on for that.
1985	30	Got married. Started work at a steel company, part of a large industrial group	During my MBA year I met my wife and we were married early in 1985. We then moved to what was the Transvaal for my new job
1986	31		
1987	32		I was not happy at the steel company, the politics was very harsh.
1988	33	Was transferred to a pharmaceutical company, part of the same group	I got a transfer to a company in the same group
1989	34	Was seconded to the SA office of a large international banking group	An opportunity came up for a secondment to an international bank
1990	35		
1991	36	Returned to the head office of the large industrial group to head up their corporate university.	I had the opportunity to meet executives and academics from around the world. Did some good work setting up the training of managers.
1992	37	The function was unbundled into a subsidiary company	I had a strong and immediate personality clash with the managing director of the business unit.
1993	38	Took retrenchment and started my own consulting business	This was a very empowering time.

It is useful to do this first for the major dates – when you moved towns; when you finished school; post-school study dates; marriage; your first child; job changes etc. Go up and down the sheet several times, and dredge memories out from the recesses of your mind. You may need to check dates. Write as much detail as you can. This can take quite some time. If you have not done this sort of activity before, you may want to do it over a period of a few days, so that you get the facts right and think through why each recorded event is significant. It's amazing how many events get lost in everyday business.

6. I then move on to the last column and comment on what the information on my timeline tells me. I discovered a regular 20-year cycle in my timeline.

There are no hard-and-fast rules for this section. What does the information in your timeline tell you? Can you see burning platforms, endings, neutral zones, new beginnings? Do you change jobs at predictable intervals? Was there one (or more) massive life-changing event that caused a complete break from your previous life? When did significant relationships take place and when did they end? What are the great 'endings'?

7. I place asterisks (*) at the watershed moments. I look at the preceding events and the following events, and recognise the patterns they form.

    I mark the happy times and the not-so-happy times in green and blue highlighter respectively. Take note how these times tie in with other events happening in your life at that time. Examine whether they follow in sequence, or if they are bunched together in a particular array.

8. I identify which times and events I would like to do over if I had a chance, specifically those that I want to get right the second time around. I highlight these in yellow.

Once you have all this down, give it a day or two to stew in your mind. You may recall forgotten events. Connections between events may now become obvious for the first time. Dwell on it. Painful recollections, long suppressed, may surface. That is all right. Give yourself time to engage fully with the hurt and the joy of this collection of events that is your life.

Activity 4 – Create Your Timeline

Write up your own timeline. You may have to make several attempts. Long-forgotten issues may emerge. That's fine, it's the thinking about them that's important.

5.1.2 Consolidating the timeline

What is your timeline telling you?

- Do you see trends repeating themselves?
- Do you make similar mistakes regularly?
- Is there a pattern of good or failed relationships?
- What are your great achievements (according to your own understanding of achievements)?
- Why do you regard those achievements as great? Explain the rationale to yourself.
- When have you experienced profound personal growth?
- When have you done an about turn and tried something else?

You can do this exercise alone, with a loved one, a spouse, a life partner or a trusted friend. Try to find the answers to these questions and capture them in a way that's accessible to you. The important thing is to ensure that you deal with your life, your needs and your dreams. You may have to write up several iterations of your timeline, as forgotten memories resurface.

Step back when you have it all down. Absorb it. It's pretty impressive, isn't it? There has been a lot going on in your life. It's all down there in front of you, in summary form.

5.2 Life ambitions

Got all that done? Let us move on. Now comes the tricky part. Mull over the following three questions:

1. What should you leave behind?

    - Are there goals that you set yourself, which now are no longer realistic?
    - What relationships no longer work for you? Should you walk away?
    - What aspirations are no longer achievable? Remember the astronaut or the climb up Mount Everest.
    - Are there things you wanted to do, but could not afford?

2. What do you want to take with you?

    - What are the things you can, and still want, to achieve?
    - What new aspirations have emerged?
    - Have you had a long-felt urge to do something quite simple, but haven't got around to it? Write a book; spend a week on the Garden Route; climb a local hill; bake a cake?

3. What is there still to do?

    - Is there unfinished business?
    - Is there a life task you still have to achieve? Are there unfulfilled goals to reach – or one that you are in the process of reaching?

This will take some time, so write this down. It helps to think of this as a sorting exercise, putting your ambitions into a choice of three 'boxes', the first called 'Leave Behind', a second labelled 'Take With Me', and a third called 'Still To Do'.

Chapter 5: Evaluation

Leave Behind	Take With Me	Still To Do

Take Action Now!

Activity 5 – Life Ambitions

Write up your Life Ambitions Worksheet. You may want to return to it, add to it and think about it. You can use your journal or the worksheet provided above. You may privately be revisiting these from time to time as new insights emerge. Do not forget about those ten empty lines at the end of your timeline – they're for the Still to Do!

Many people report a great sense of relief once they have captured the Leave Behind items. One person I know hand-wrote them on a piece of paper, and buried it in the garden as a symbolic closure ritual.

If you find that you have an extremely long list under Still to Do, pause and think about it. Are you being realistic about what you can achieve? Has too much unfinished business accumulated in your life? The open door is only big enough for one person's baggage.

Share this process with someone who has known you for a long time. They may add different insights, and also point out issues that you are uncomfortable about facing.

Something to watch out for at this point: It is easy to arrive at a quick, simple solution. It goes like this: "I see the trends. I see what has worked. I see what went wrong. What I need to do is …" Don't be tempted to go off on a sudden quick fix!

One of my early ambitions was to be a 'great person' in

the world of business. A CEO, an MD, or someone with a similarly grand-sounding title. Through a process of drawing a number of different timelines and reflecting on them, and coming to understand the underlying structures, I realised I had an inappropriate temperament for the role of CEO of an organisation. I don't work well in teams, I don't enjoy working within rules and boundaries, and I lack the ruthless ambition to be the 'man in the corner office'. I took a different route and I have not regretted it.

5.2.1 The 'bucket list'

Before we go on to the next topic, let's exchange a few more thoughts about the bucket list, a term that has passed into common usage. We touched on it when we discussed midlife.

The term 'bucket list' comes from the movie of the same name, but the notion is much older than that. To summarise the content of the movie for those who are not familiar with it:

> Two men in the last quarter of their lives suddenly seize upon all the things they wanted to do but never did. They write a list of actions they want to complete before they kick the bucket (hence the 'bucket list'). They then go off and do the activities on the list. It helps that one of the two men in the movie is extremely wealthy and can afford to support both participants.

The idea is that if you don't do all the things on your bucket list, you will be unfulfilled and that somehow you will have wasted your life. Don't buy into this misconception.

While this is powerful stuff for a movie, it usually does not play out in real life. It's very easy to be seduced by the allure of a bucket list. This is a list of things you have to do, achieve, experience, because if you don't, your life will remain somehow incomplete. Besides, you and I don't necessarily have the support of a wealthy friend.

I'm not referring to the 'should do' things – like making peace with a relative from whom you are estranged or cleaning out the accumulated junk in your garage rather than leaving that job to your heirs. These sorts of lists are necessary.

If you have made a bucket list, consider it carefully:

- Are these goals important to you, or are they activities you wish to undertake for the benefit of your friends and relatives, that they might admire you? – *Swim with dolphins?*
- Do these goals hang over from another time when you were a different person in different circumstances? – *Skydiving?*
- Have you set this goal to boost your ego or self-esteem? – *Visit 100 countries?*

What happens when you have accomplished everything on your bucket list and you are still empty?

One way of assessing whether your bucket list is there for the right reasons is to ask yourself this question: Have you told everyone about it, or is it an inner personal journey?

If all your friends and relatives know about your bucket list – and you remind them regularly of it – then you are probably doing it for the wrong reasons. Put the bucket list aside and be the best friend and relative to your family and close circle of friends that you can be. They will honour you more for that.

By now, your personal burning platform will probably have fully emerged. You may feel the discomfort. You vacillate between clinging to the old and familiar, and reaching out to the new and uncharted. The challenge of experiencing a burning platform is that once you recognise it, nothing is the same again. Be strong. We are not finished.

5.3 The 'Circle of Influence'

This exercise examines the different planes of influence operating in your current stage of life. There are four levels:

- *You*: This deals with you – the person. Who are you? How do you regard yourself? Your self-appreciation.
- *Your immediate circle*: This group includes the people you deal with every day. Your spouse or life partner. Your family. Your close friends. Your good work colleagues. You know these people well and they know you well.
- *Your wider circle*: This is the wider circle of acquaintances. You do not have as much closeness with these people. They could be neighbours, old school friends, your boss's boss (if you have one). These people know you, but they are somewhat remote.
- *Out there*: This is the wider community. It may be an industry association you serve on, or the folk at the public library, or a charity you assist.

5.3.1 Me

Begin with yourself and have the following conversation:

- What do I like about myself?
- What do I believe other people think of me?
- What is my personality? Avoid labels like 'extroversion' and 'introversion' and if you are stuck, use the list of adjectives in the resources section at the end of this book to find words that best describe you. Narrow the list down to ten adjectives. You do not need to rank or sort them. What does this list tell you? Do you like this person? Do you want to spend the rest of your life with this person?
- Then look at the list of adjectives in the resources section again and select the most appropriate adjectives you would ideally like to describe yourself.

- Put the two lists together.
- How much do they overlap?
- If they are similar – good!
- If they diverge significantly, there is lots of work to do.

Take Action Now!

Activity 6 – Adjectives that Best Describe You

Compile your list of adjectives.

5.3.2 My immediate circle

Now let's look at your immediate circle. This includes family, close friends and close work colleagues. They are lumped together because you spend most of your time with these people. They have shaped you and you have shaped them.

What have you contributed to this group? How have you made their lives easier or more enjoyable? What have you given them? Do this in the context of individuals rather than an institution. List what you have given to a person. Being a father. Talking to your daughter about life. Being a good wife and equal life partner. Being a supportive brother or sister. What have you given to the people in your immediate circle: support, advice, problem solving, etc.?

What was your contribution? What should you have given? What would you have liked to have given but didn't?

If the people in this group came together over lunch in a local restaurant, what would they say about you? This is tough, isn't it!

5.3.3 My wider influence

Cast the net wider to include acquaintances that you meet in passing or at work. People who are not friends, but who nevertheless have interacted with you. These people could be:

- Colleagues at work
- Members of a committee you served on
- Other parents on a school governing body
- Supporters of a club, church or association.

You know the drill now. What have you contributed? What have you given? What should you have given? What would you have liked to have given but did not?

5.3.4 Out there

This one is more difficult. What was your contribution to the broader community?

If you have nothing to record here, that is quite all right.

Activity 7 – Circle of Influence

Take Action Now!

Write up your Circle of Influence, starting with You. It's not as easy as it looks.

5.4 Summary

As we come to the end of this section, let's review what we have achieved so far:

- You have your *timeline*: Insight on the trends and patterns in your life. How well have you lived your life?
- You have your *life ambitions*: The three boxes – 'Leave Behind', 'Take with Me' and 'Still to Do'. What do you take

Chapter 5: Evaluation

with you and what do you leave behind for the next phase of your life?

- You have your *circle of influence*: Your impact on your world. What is your contribution to the world?

Together they will allow you to triangulate, much as a land surveyor does, your life path.

Activity 8 – Journal Notes

Make notes in your journal. Everybody I know who reaches this point writes down reams of understandings, viewpoints and revelations. Don't hold back. Get it all out. This is a special moment in the process. Take your time. You are communicating deeply with yourself.

In the next section, as you forge ahead into the next phase of your life, we begin exploring the following:

- How can I avoid repeating past mistakes?
- What important tasks do I take forward to my future?
- How can I use my past contributions?

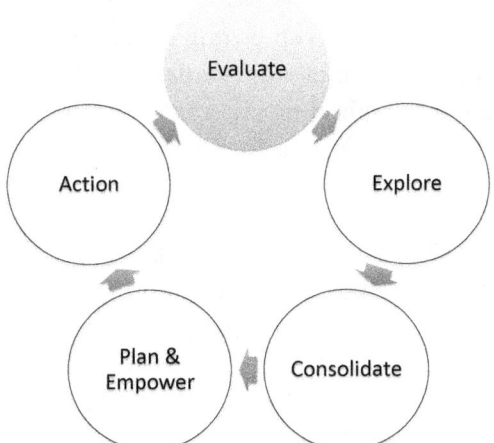

If you thought it was tough up until here, the going gets tougher. Here is the progress chart thus far.

It's time to go exploring!

69

5.5 Case Study: Sandra – afraid to jump!

Sandra was in her mid-forties when all this started. She is driven, and a perfectionist who has to be highly organised. She has a string of higher qualifications, and she is razor intelligent. She grew up in a home where she was the less favoured, less attractive sister. Consequently she had to work so much harder to outshine her sister and win her parents' approval.

Sandra was a teacher for the early part of her career. She was very good at this. She always got through the curriculum on time, and her administration was consistently up to date. But she became bored with teaching. It was the same thing year after year, just different children. (Recognise the settled neural pathways?) She had optimised her systems and teaching materials to the point that any improvement would be negligible. She needed a change, and she set out to see how she could move laterally.

Through utilising her contacts, she secured the position of librarian in the archive of a major corporation. She was an excellent performer. Her personality suited the highly structured environment. She even dabbled in some training. Soon she was undertaking more and more training programmes within the organisation – her skills as a teacher were standing her in good stead. She even began designing training programmes. The environment was similar to what she had known in teaching but she had much greater freedom. She was not too fazed when feedback described her as directive and inflexible.

The inevitable organisational restructure came, but Sandra was able to secure a contract with her erstwhile employer. All was well until a new CEO arrived and the organisation cut back on its training activities. To compound the problem, her husband was also retrenched by his employer. They had to drastically rework their lifestyle and priorities.

Chapter 5: Evaluation

Based on the strength of her experience and references, Sandra obtained work as a trainer and facilitator with another, much smaller but more creative organisation in the same industry. This didn't work out because Sandra was too rigid in her approach and was unable to adapt to a more flexible style of training delivery and work performance.

Sandra now does sporadic contract work. She doesn't develop long-term relationships with her clients because she is too forthright in telling them about their operational deficiencies. She is unhappy and feels that the world has turned against her.

What can we learn from Sandra's situation?

- Sandra was behaviourally inflexible and was unable to adapt to changing circumstances.
- She failed to plan and consequently was looking for roles that suited her style, rather than adapting her style to suit a wider range of organisations.
- Sandra failed to build a support network around her to help her transition into a more flexible approach to work.
- She couldn't let go and make the decisions to change herself, and grow into a new, more fulfilling role. Sandra did not have a clear idea of what she wanted for herself. Consequently she did not know what to look for.

If we rephrase Sandra's situation into positive midlife learnings:

- The world changes continually. An empowered midlife demands behavioural flexibility in order to adapt to the changed circumstances.
- Planning for a stimulating and rewarding second half means finding situations that stretch and change you beneficially.

71

- You always need a support network around you. It's never too early to start.
- It starts with taking the decision to change yourself into a more fulfilled and contented person.

These days Sandra is in her late fifties. Her friends are put off by her negative outlook on life. She blames others because she has not found her niche.

Chapter 6

Exploration

What is needed, rather than running away or controlling or suppressing or any other resistance, is understanding fear; that means, watch it, learn about it, come directly into contact with it. We are to learn about fear, not how to escape from it.
— Jiddu Krishnamurti

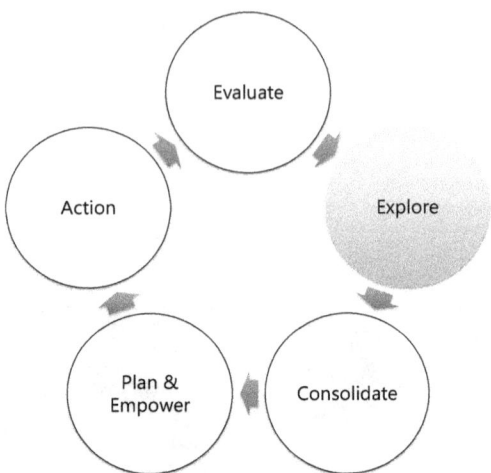

Now you have your back story, you have an understanding of where you have come from and you understand what and how life events have shaped you.

In the same way that a competition diver uses a diving board to launch into open space, we explore how your life experiences thus far have given you the wisdom and skills for the great task that lies before you. It is going to catapult you into your best possible future.

6.1 What is your Happiness Base?

Your timeline is a good place to start.

Go back over your timeline and find those stages on the timeline when you were happiest and most fulfilled. This should be very familiar as by now you have been up and down your timeline several times. Make notes about what you were doing at each of those times by answering the questions in the following worksheet:

Chapter 6: Exploration

Timeline stage: _____		
Question	**Answer**	**Rank**
(1) What friendships did you have?		
(2) What workplace skills and achievements were most satisfying to you?		
(3) What was your work situation?		
(4) What recreational activities did you enjoy?		
(5) What was your social life like?		
(6) Were you creative in art or music?		
(7) Were you making things with your hands and with tools?		
(8) What was happening in your spiritual life?		
(9) Were you leading or participating in groups of people?		
(10) Were you mainly alone and solitary?		

Then rank the answers to these ten questions starting with the most rewarding activity you experienced to the least rewarding. Rank them from one to ten:

1, 2, 3, 4, 5, 6, 7, 8, 9, 10.

If two or more activities were equally rewarding, give them the same number and adjust the subsequent numbers accordingly:

1, 2, 2, 4, 5, 6, 7, 8, 9, 10.

Activity 9 – Happiness Base

Write up your Happiness Base worksheets. You may have several worksheets, each relating to a specific period of your life. This is time consuming, so you might want to do this over several days.

Now go to your Life Ambitions sheets and look at the 'Take With Me' and 'Still To Do' boxes.

What are the events or activities in your ranked list that resonate with your life ambitions? Are the two sets similar, or does the content differ markedly? The greater the overlap, the more depth you have already achieved. The bigger the difference, the more you still have to do. Make some notes about this in your journal or on the worksheet. Ponder over it.

Now turn to your Circle of Influence.

Start making connections, see trends, identify recurring, similar events. Good or bad life decisions, good or toxic relationships? What is the emerging picture? Make some more notes about this in your journal or on the worksheet. Think about it. Let it speak to you.

You will probably have piles of notes, squiggly lines and much to consider. This will allow you to triangulate, much as a land surveyor does, your life story.

Chapter 6: Exploration

Activity 10 – Write up Journal

Write up the new insights in your journal. Sometimes it helps to create diagrams showing the relationship between the various components. There are no rules for this. It is going to look messy. But you will be aware of what is unfolding.

6.2 Exploring the unknown

Now you have some ideas to enable you to explore options.

Your focus changes now. You take the insights you have gathered about yourself and begin looking outwards. Perhaps something new, a path or position, begins to suggest itself from all you have written in your journal and in the worksheets.

Most of the time there are two options:

- You have a reasonably clear understanding of what to attempt.
- There are so many options that you cannot make up your mind.

Don't rush it – you need to take time to think about this. It's not a quick fix. Don't forget, your brain is quietly rewiring in the background!

Some things to keep in mind are:

- Do I gradually work my way into this new role?
- Do I make a sudden clean break, and walk away from my current situation?
- Will I have to move towns or give up precious relationships?
- Will I have to spend a great deal of time or money to set myself up for my new adventure?

You will go through phases. You may become enamoured with a particular course of action. However, the next day you may change your mind. This is how it goes.

6.2.1 Using the internet

We live in the era of the internet search engine. Assuming you are a competent internet user, you know your way around finding information on the net. This is an impressive source of unlimited information about nearly everything.

Spend a weekend or two researching the life and work options you are considering. Explore new ideas. Make a list of the topics, the choices, the careers, the hobbies you're interested in and investigate them. Cut and paste, or write them up in a mini research document. Put down all the details. Open up a Pinterest board with pictures of the things you would like or want to do, or the places you're keen to visit. Conduct a wide search. Don't limit yourself. This might just be the moment when you stumble onto something new and life-changing.

Don't go about this aimlessly. Build up a portfolio of evidence. Keep records of the sites you visit. Print out documents or save them into categorised folders. Evernote™ is very useful for this. Write up your notes as you go along. Make summaries. Treat it like a school theme project or a master's dissertation.

Activity 11 – Web Research

Off you go! Dig around. Keep a record of the sites you visit. You will discover information about resources, processes, tools, training, skills and a host of other requirements. Read actively and make notes as they pertain to your personal situation.

6.2.2 Your pool of Wise Folks

Once you have researched some ideas and conceptualised a few possibilities, it is time to speak to friends whose judgement you trust. A lot can be gained from close friends who have knowledge or experience of the areas you are interested in. Discuss the topics with them.

Activity 12 – Wise Folks

Make a list of Wise Folks and talk to them. Find practitioners who are doing the things that you want to do. Pal up to them and find out how they go about it. Buy them breakfast and pick their brains. You have no idea how much information a good breakfast can buy.

6.3 Finding the connections

Review the information you have before you. There should be some sort of connection or extrapolation from your past into your desired future. You may want to use your skills in a different manner. If you were a construction manager, you might consider a part-time project manager job with an NGO.

On the other hand, you may have taken art as a school subject, but never had the opportunity to go on with it. Perhaps art is unfinished business. You might take art lessons. Or you might get a drawing book and a range of pencils and decide whether the old passion is still there.

You may have spent your working career in an office in a high-rise building. Now you want to grow vegetables. Perhaps convert your back garden, or transform the balcony of your flat to suit that purpose.

You have a vast amount of experience and skill. The problem is that we discount those skills. In our minds we assume that everyone can do the things we can do. We touched on this earlier.

Well, here is news for you. Very few people have the mix of skills and experience that you have. There are organisations out there that are desperate for your specific skills set. You just have to find them.

Activity 13 – Do the Work!

Take Action Now!

There are no worksheets or tools for this. Write it up in any form that works for you. Play with the information. Your head may say one thing, your heart another. Follow the options and objections.

Things to consider:

- You may be in a high-powered job (or not quite so high-powered) and you loathe it. You want to get out. You are doing things and taking decisions that you detest. You are hanging in only for the pension.

- You may be in a situation where you have to continue in your day job because you need the income stream. Your opportunity lies in exploring the opportunities outside working hours. Instead of watching television in the evenings or on the weekends, you can start doing new activities to transition yourself.

- Some of you might have already retired, and are bored. Well then, you can get stuck in straight away.

- You may have been retrenched and are in desperate need of an income. Well, with downsizing you can explore the next career. (I have been retrenched twice in my life.)

A caveat: If what you want to do is way off the mark from what you are doing now, it means you may have been in the wrong job or wrong situation for most of your life. This is a very sad situation because it means you have been living someone else's dream.

In practice, what you want to become and who you are now will differ by degree and intensity but will not usually be diametrically opposed.

Example: If you have never sailed a keelboat before, think very carefully about selling your home and buying a keelboat to sail around the world. You might be a bit too old to learn the skills required. Maybe you can sail a dinghy on a dam? Or build radio-controlled model boats? There are different routes to the same satisfaction.

I always wanted to own a game farm. I imagined sitting in the late afternoon and watching the sun set as I looked out over the plains of Africa. However – reality check – I realised that this would never come about. So I built a small lapa[ii] at the bottom of my garden and I enjoy sitting there of an evening and watching the fire burn down – exactly as I would have done if I had owned a game farm.

6.4 Summary

By now it should be clear. You are about to jump off the burning platform. It is getting hot and you are itching to go!

Your internal conversation may be as follows:

- I could never afford that.
- If I did that, we would have to move to a different town. The family would never support that.
- I do not have the skills to do that.
- That is a job/role/hobby for a young person.
- I am a bit scared.

---

ii An open-sided structure often used for entertainment purposes. Perhaps an African summer house without glass windows? My lapa is made out of wooden laths.

Midlife Renewal: Unlock the Hidden Door

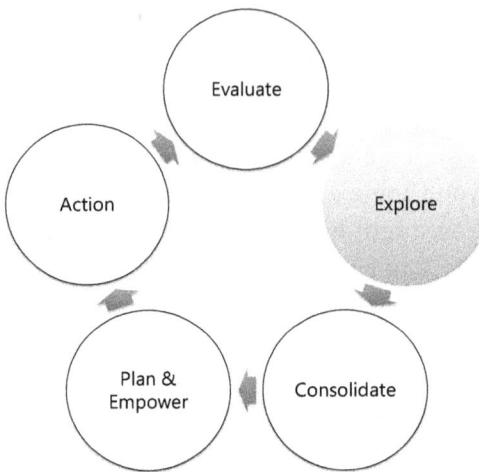

Hold back on the negatives. We are getting towards describing the ideal state. Later we will get to what is practical and achievable.

You have come to the end of the Exploration phase. You have lots of new and exciting, maybe even frightening ideas.

In the next section we will consolidate them into clearly defined options so that you can take the best decisions for yourself and your loved ones.

6.5 Case Study: Simphiwe the entrepreneur

Simphiwe is a qualified accountant. He has a relaxed, urbane style and is well liked. He spent his entire early working career in a state-owned company. At an early age, he achieved the career goal he had set for himself when he left university. His position had considerable status and his duties took him on business trips to all parts of the world. He drove a large German-made car and had all the latest business devices and gadgets. His wife had elegant gifts from New York and Milan, much to the envy of their friends. To most, Simphiwe had achieved the ultimate in a successful life.

The only problem was that Simphiwe was deeply unhappy. He found the stultified, slow-moving culture of the organisation deeply frustrating. Those darn pathways in the brain! The office politics was upsetting. In spite of all the outer trappings of success, he felt deeply unfulfilled. He wanted to have greater freedom and put his skills and experience to better use.

Simphiwe and his wife began talking this over, and started putting forward various options and ideas. Simphiwe's wife has an advanced degree in economics, and so it was a natural progression for them to start a financial services advisory firm. At first it started small, running from home. Simphiwe assisted in the evening when he got home. This was demanding, but they were both enthusiastic about the venture. They downsized their lifestyle and set aside funding for the business. They had a joint goal.

Eventually the business grew in size to the point where they took modest offices in a nearby office park. After much deliberation and not a little anxiety, Simphiwe resigned from his job and worked full time in the family business. To their surprise, Simphiwe's former employer offered them a series of assignments very similar to the work he had been performing. This was a great help in putting the business on a sound financial footing.

Today Simphiwe and his wife are running a flourishing small business. They have none of the status or perks of his former job, but they love the freedom and creativity of being in their own business.

Simphiwe's learnings from this experience:

- Don't burn your bridges with your former employer.
- It is ok to live modestly.
- The skills you use in your current job can be your springboard to the next.
- You have to discuss and agree on important life changes with your spouse or partner.
- Success is what you consider to be success. Don't try to be successful on someone else's terms.

- Don't put up with a job you don't like just because it pays a good salary.
- It takes time for your dreams to come true. Don't divert from the plan.
- When you leave your old job, inform all your business acquaintances. They are often able to provide leads or work opportunities.

Chapter 7

Consolidation

Change is such hard work.
Billy Crystal

Midlife Renewal: Unlock the Hidden Door

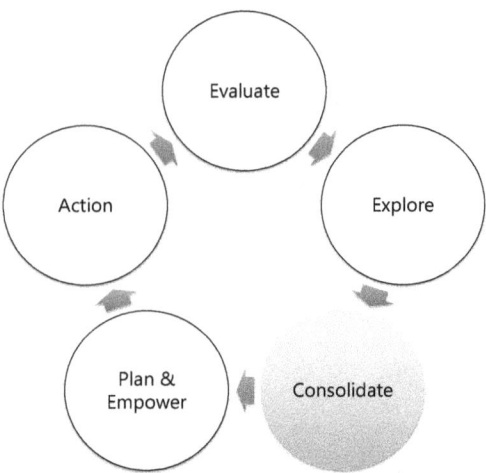

This is where it comes together. Tie together the strands of what you have uncovered about yourself and the person you wish to become.

The situation might look like the following:

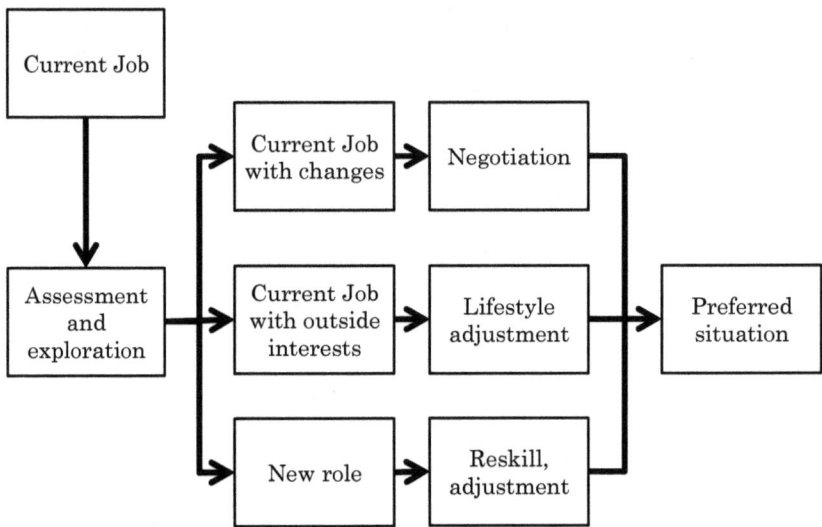

At the risk of oversimplifying the matter, there are three options open to you:

Option to be Pursued	Fulfilment Action
Current role with changes *You can stay in your current role or job, and restructure it so that it meets your changed needs and aspirations.*	You will negotiate changes with the organisation for which you work. *This is the least risky option.*
Current role with outside interests *You may be satisfied with your current job or role, or locked in because of financial considerations. You can explore your new interest outside of your current job or role through a hobby or craft, a sport or involvement in an after-hours organisation.*	**You will find other outside interests that give you fulfilment.** *This is slightly more risky than the previous option, but still relatively easy to undertake.*
New role *Your current situation may be of such a nature that you want to escape it entirely. Or you may have the financial resources that will allow you to make a clean break.*	**You will have to learn and put into practice new skills in a new role.** *This is the most risky as you may not be able to resume your earlier position if things do not work out. It calls for careful consideration.*

Before taking weighty decisions scope what you have uncovered and evaluate the options.

7.1 Pulling it together

The consolidation process is awkward. A voice in your head says: "You can't go off and do something else. You have responsibilities."

These voices from the past resound in your head:

- What your mother always told you.
- What your father always told you.
- What your wife or your husband told you.
- What your boss told you to do to be accepted and achieve the things you strive for.
- You might have had a father who said, "Music will never be a career. You cannot do music."
- Your wife might say, "You cannot grow a beard. It looks ugly and what will the neighbours say?"
- You might have a husband who says, "You want to go back to university to study law? You have a perfectly good life here."

These are not real barriers. They are accumulated messages absorbed over your life. If you are to find the open door, you have to tame these messages and get them under control. That brain thing again. Identify each of these invisible barriers. Get to know them, understand them and test each one against your plan:

- Consider each objection to your proposed new life.
- Determine which part of your plan the objection affects.
- Go back to the corresponding position on the timeline, the life ambitions and the circle of influence. If it means you break a previous negative emotional or relationship spiral, then you are on the right track.

We will identify these and break each one of these invisible chains that hold you back. They are stopping you from becoming who you want to be.

You are in the second half of your life. Time is running out. You don't have unlimited time. Think carefully before you abandon something because you think it is impractical.

Chapter 7: Consolidation

You may want to be a saxophone player in a jazz band. What 55-year-old woman plays in a jazz band when she should be looking after grandchildren and keeping house?

That is an excellent reason to be playing the saxophone in a jazz band.

Now we are going to write up the 'big picture'. This is the 'business case' for what you want to do. Draw on the worksheets and journal and begin creating the big picture for each of your options. The following worksheet is supplied to assist you.

Big picture questions	Option 1	Option 2
Describe the end state you want to achieve.		
Describe how you will get there: • What are the action steps? • What will you do? • What will others do? • How will you persuade them to assist you?		
Describe what you need to buy (equipment, licences, resources, skills, etc.)		
Describe what new information you need to learn (background information, theory, etc.)		
Describe what new skills you need to be trained in (equipment, software, etc.)		

89

Activity 14 – Personal Business Case

Write up your personal business case in a format that makes sense to you. You can keep it short and succinct, or you can go deep and explain the reasoning behind each action. This is up to you and for you. Do it in such a way that it suits you and can best be used by you.

7.2 Impact on your immediate circle

Test out your proposed courses of action on your immediate circle. Even if you have involved them along the way, you will still need to test it with them. They may not have realised your commitment to a course of action. Remember, we discussed how different people go at different speeds from Endings to New Beginnings (section 2.1).

- Listen to their reactions. What are they telling you?
- Are there any deal-breakers? Any ultimatums?
- Will you have to sever longstanding or important relationships?
- Is there another way?

Bear in mind that they are also going through their own change and transition process brought about by your decisions. Perhaps they don't share the same burning platform with you. Or maybe they have their own set of complex endings to deal with. Be sensitive. Spend lots of time talking it through. Debate it, rather than present it as a *fait accompli*. Ask for advice. Understand how it will affect them by asking questions. Don't rush to a conclusion.

7.3 For love or money?

Each of your proposed courses of action requires you to consider the following:

- Are you expecting to be remunerated for this new venture, or are you going to fund it yourself? How much are you expecting to make/spend?
- If you are expecting remuneration, prepare a detailed business case. This outlines the actions, costs, income and timing to see if you can afford your new venture.
- If you do not expect to receive remuneration, review your other income streams. If you have passive income streams, can they support you and your dependants?
- If you have to maintain active income streams, have you the time and energy to attend to both?

Do not underestimate the cash flow implications of suddenly resigning from a job that guarantees a regular – if very small – income. Keep your eggs uncracked and safe in your basket.

7.4 Training and preparation

Depending on the options chosen, you may have to learn new skills. If you have been a lawyer all your life, and you want to go into designing mobile apps, you are likely to need specialised training over and above the range of skills you have already gathered. What additional training, skills or preparation do you require?

Your internal dialogue may go something like this:

- Do I have unfinished business?
- Do I have a calling for a particular vocation?
- Can I remedy previous bad decisions regarding career and life decisions?
- What is the balance between reality and dreams?
- Do I want to write a book?
- Do I want special time with my grandchildren?

- Do I want to go cycling across Europe?
- Will I need a bigger garage to accommodate my new tools/equipment?
- Will I need a smaller home to save costs?

Some of your options may require participation in formal training courses; some of the skills can be picked up by working alongside experts; some you will just pick up through trial and error. You don't always have to pay for training. For example, you could give consulting time to a client in exchange for free attendance on a specialised technical training programme. The beauty of barter is that it is off the balance sheet and non-taxable.

You may need new equipment or other resources to move ahead and you may need to make changes to your existing infrastructure.

If you write your responses on little 'Post-It' notes, you can cluster them and move them around. See what goes together, and what combinations result in conflict over resources or other obligations. Then use the worksheet below to create a Resource Plan of what you have to do, and how much it will cost. Do this for each of your career options.

	Costs	**Timing**
Training		
Equipment		
Other Resources		
Employment		

What you have in front of you now is a plan from which you will create the rest of your career and the rest of your life.

Activity 15 – Resource Plan

Write up your Resource Plan. Capture your workings and assumptions. Work out the month-by-month cash-flow implications. How much is it going to cost in MONEY? How much will it cost in TIME?

In all likelihood you will have clusters of activities that amplify or re-purpose your current skill and experience set. This is good. You may want to deploy your knowledge of tax and accounting in an artistic direction. You might have been an electrician, and now you want to do art, using wiring diagrams as a departure concept.

Use an internet search engine to gain more detailed information about the choices and options you are considering.

In some cases you will be able to move from one career into another with relatively little retraining and with little loss of income. For most of us however, going from one career into another is not always a viable alternative and so we have to continue with a job for survival while in the background we slowly groom ourselves for the new job. We do this by undergoing training courses, reading up about it, and trying out the new skill. We jam with the jazz band. We read up about the stock market. We learn about how to become a blacksmith, plumber, carpenter or investment adviser by talking to and watching people in these professions.

Once you have investigated and analysed two or three career renewal options, assess how practical it is to make the move. Look at the gap between where you are now and where you need to be. Ascertain what you need to learn, to buy, to own, and to borrow. In some cases you may try talking to someone at the company you currently work for. Perhaps there are openings and opportunities in line with your career renewal options for which you can be considered.

7.5 The Big Decision

Yes, that's right. If you have not already done so, you will now have to make a decision. The decision.

Perhaps you have already subliminally made your decision, or the facts have convinced you. You will know where you stand on the change and transition continuum.

You might have realised that you are quite content with where you are and that no midlife changes are required. If that is the case, please don't close this book. You can adapt the remainder of this process to map out what you are going to do in the context of your current situation.

For those of you who want to move away from the life you currently have, it is decision time. If you are not ready to take the decision – which is different from deciding not to embark on midlife renewal – take a break. Put the plans and notes and worksheets to one side and do something else. Spend the weekend away. Go for a walk. Work in the garden. Arrange a family dinner. You will know when you are ready to resume the journey, and make your big decision, in whichever direction it takes you.

7.6 Summary

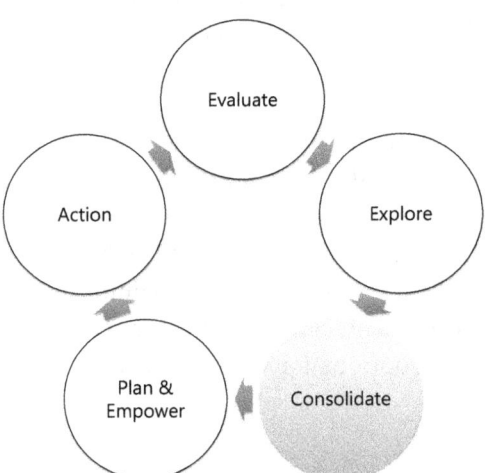

This is the end of consolidating the various options. In the next phase we look at what can be done to make these options a reality.

7.6 Case Study: Creative Lindiwe

Lindiwe is a competent, personable, middle-aged person. Her early career started in a listed company in various mid-management roles. She was exposed to all facets of the business and built up a sound repertoire of business skills. She then relocated to a government department because her skill set matched the requirements in that new role. She found this very stressful as she felt that she was required to carry both inexperienced subordinates and inefficient supervisors. She felt that she was having to do several jobs at once: helping an incompetent boss perform in his role, and micro-manage a set of subordinates who lacked skills and enthusiasm.

Lindiwe was becoming more and more disillusioned about the role of government, and more and more unhappy about her own career. She felt she was stagnating and not paying sufficient attention to her own development. While in this highly frustrating role, she was head-hunted by another well-known and established private company. She accepted this with alacrity, as this promised to be the answer to her current situation.

She quickly found that things were not as she expected in the new company. There was an immediate clash of values, which had not been apparent during the recruiting process. It was a highly controlling environment, with scant regard for the individuals in the organisation. The sole measure of personal worth was achievement of aggressive sales targets.

At this time Lindiwe was a single mother, and the long hours and lack of appreciation at work were taking a toll on her health and her relationship with her young son.

One day it just got too much. She resigned. This was uncharacteristic as Lindiwe is a careful planner. She had no idea what she was going to do or where she was going to go.

She just walked out because she didn't want to put up with the highly toxic environment any more.

After she had spent two weeks at home walking around the house in her pyjamas and drinking far too much coffee, she began to get back in control of her life. She spoke to her financial adviser about her financial situation, and what lifestyle changes she should be undertaking. This turned out to be a masterstroke. The adviser was a tremendous help, not only with revising her expenses, but assisting her with planning the next stage of her life.

She owned a rental property that she had purchased earlier in her career. She now set about re-modelling and improving the asset, and then sold it. With the proceeds she began an art and *objets d'art* business, which was an evolutionary migration from the home renovation activities.

Soon she was running a small and moderately successful art dealership. This was diametrically opposed to her previous corporate life, but she loved it. Dealing with artistic people, persuading customers and just appreciating good art was intensely satisfying. It gave Lindiwe a sense that she could accomplish anything, and that she had a set of sound human and business skills. It also enabled her to network with her work and social acquaintances in a different context. She found that some of these acquaintances began approaching her to find out how she had transformed her life because they were experiencing personal or work difficulties. Lindiwe embraced this fully and found she has a great aptitude for coaching and life support. She enjoyed this so much that the she signed up and completed an international coaching qualification. While she was balancing the demands of the art business and her emerging coaching business, she was approached by a business and coaching consultancy regarding an assignment that required coaching and also required her earlier corporate expertise.

Chapter 7: Consolidation

This turned out to be an excellent opportunity. Today Lindiwe is a valued director and shareholder in the business and is thoroughly fulfilled in the work she does.

 Lindiwe's learnings from this experience:

- Financial planning in support of your life goals is critical.

- Create more than one income stream – house rental and art in her case. You don't necessarily have to own an art gallery – you can work in one!

- Her experience in the art business made her realise that she could be successful in any endeavour she was interested in.

- Continuous development is critical. She reskilled herself in home renovation, art dealing and coaching.

- Make sure that you have a support network. In Lindiwe's case it was her financial adviser, her son and her parents. She could bounce ideas off them and they were a source of encouragement.

- Online learning is often free and can be convenient for expanding your knowledge.

- Get the balance right between hard work, family time and personal time.

- Don't stress when business is quiet. Prepare and self-develop during the quiet times so as to be ready for opportunities when they arise. They will happen.

Chapter 8

Planning and Empowering

It may be hard for an egg to turn into a bird: it would be a jolly sight harder for it to learn to fly while remaining an egg.
C. S. Lewis

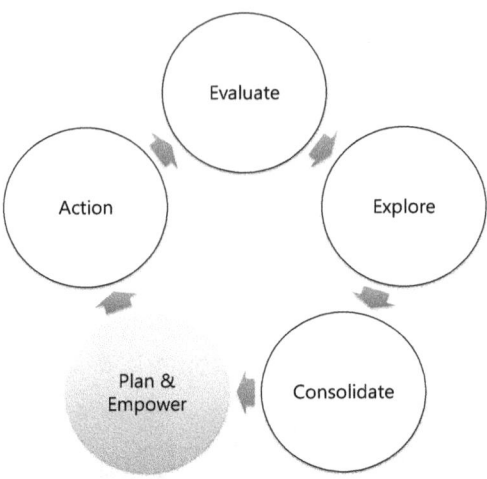

8.1 Where to start?

The planning and empowering is the fun part. You should be experiencing some sort of relief in seeing a clearer picture of your midlife phase, and you should be excited and energised by the possibilities of your future. It is a bit like applying for your first job with all the accompanying fear and anticipation.

This section puts together your Personalised Action Plan.

Many of you have a strong background in various types of project management. These skills may come from running a family or from work experience. After all, you haven't reached midlife without bashing out a project or two. All of us got things done whether at work or at home. If you run a household, you are an expert in project management. I am going to share some ideas, but you are sure to have your own approach. Let's see how we go.

Do this on your dining room table (I am assuming you have a rectangular dining room table – an oval one will work just as well):

- *Step 1*: First, describe how your life will appear after the successful implementation of your renewal. Describe it in detail – what you do, where you do it, what relationships you are in. Write it down on a sheet of A4 paper and place it on the right-hand edge of your dining room table. That is 'then', where you are going. The table will look something like this image.

- *Step 2*: Note down your current state, where you are now, and place this on the left-hand edge of your dining table. This is 'now'.

- *Step 3*: List all the things you need to do in order to get there; write these activities down on A5 paper or large Post-Its.

- *Step 4*: Place the activities in sequence, in a straight line across the dining room table, starting with the most immediate one closest to 'now', and the last one closest to 'then'. Your dining room table might look something like the image below. All your activities will be strung across the table. At this stage they are organised equidistant from each other so that the sequence of activities looks neat. In reality some of them might be bunched up, and others may have large gaps between them.

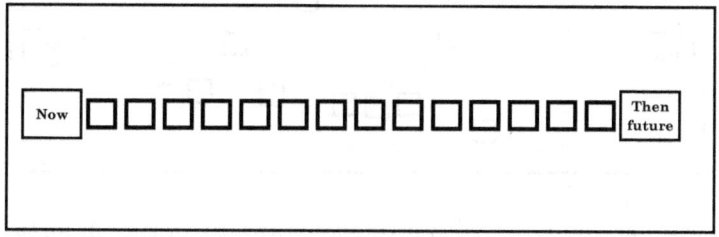

❶	Define what I want to achieve
❷	Do internet research
❸	Talk to people in the field
❹	Talk options over with a trusted friend
❺	Share with my spouse
❻	Research in public library
❼	Do some job shadowing
❽	Take two weeks' leave to work alongside folks doing similar work
❾	What new skills will I require?
❿	What are the costs?
⓫	How will I afford it?
⓬	Tell my friends
⓭	Develop an action plan
⓮	Launch my action plan

- *Step 5:* Move the cards up or down on the table depending on their importance. If the activity is relatively important move it up. If it is relatively unimportant, move it down. The dining room table should now look something like the image below.

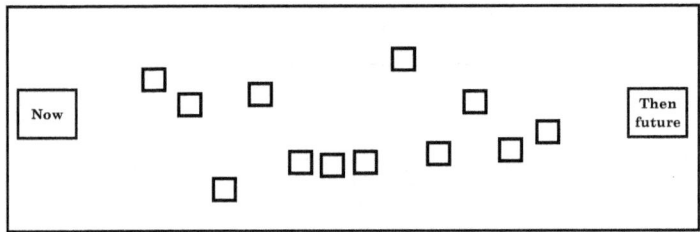

This is an action plan, with a relative ranking of the importance of each activity or stage.

Chapter 8: Planning and Empowering

Activity 16 – Action Plan

Write up your Action Plan. It is helpful to take pictures of the table once you have set up all the postings.

Those familiar with project management will know the Gantt Chart, which might look something like the one below, or it might be somewhat simpler. It sets out in visual format your renewal schedule and sets the timeframes. Use the information from your action plan and give each step a timeframe. You may discover that some activities happen simultaneously and others only occur after previous activities have taken place. Certain activities may happen at regular intervals and some of the less important tasks may be done at the same time as important tasks.

2016	March	April	May	June	July	August	September	October	November
Action 1	■								
Action 2	■								
Action 3		■	■	■	■				
Action 4		■							
Action 5				■					
Action 6						■			
Action 7		■		■				■	
Action 8							■		
Action 9							■		
Action 10								■	
Action 11									■

103

Transpose this into a more durable format. This could be:

- A double page in your journal
- A wall chart
- A spreadsheet
- A project management application/programme.

Congratulations! You have achieved a number of important goals with this exercise.

- You have described what you need to do to get to the place where you want to be.
- You have broken down the specific steps and actions you need to take to get there.
- You have set timeframes for undertaking these steps.
- You have assessed the relative importance of each action in relation to the next.

Take Action Now!

Activity 17 – Gantt Chart

Write up your Gantt Chart.

Well done! Many people go through their entire lives without having done anything close to this!

8.2 What do you need?

You have already drawn up a list of requirements in the training and preparation (section 6.4). Now is the time to get more focused. What will you have to spend money on? Make a list according to the action plan – this will be your cash outflow. Consider the following when compiling your list:

- Is there a way of getting it for free? Do you know someone who has what you are looking for and does not use it?
- Can you get it second hand? Most homes are overflowing with stuff the owners bought and that they don't use anymore. Find someone like that. The internet-based second-hand shops are very good, and a courier will deliver the item to your door.
- Can you borrow it? If you do not need something permanently, borrow it from a friend or neighbour. Or borrow it until you are competent, and then you can purchase your own item.
- What training is available and what should you choose? Who is the best value provider? Remember our earlier discussion about bartering your skills. The internet is full of good free (or very inexpensive) courses. For instance, you may consider taking a series of MOOC[iii] courses to cover ground very similar to that found in a formal programme. It's not the same as a full-time residential course of study, but it is much, much cheaper and can be done at home in your own time.
- Can you shadow someone who is in the role you want? School children go on job shadowing programmes, so why not people in their fifties? Besides, many people would take it as a compliment if you asked to shadow them for a day or two.

8.3   The support team

You need a support team, so you should let them in on your secret. Immediate family is an obvious start.

Then there's the workplace. You can access everything from time off to go to a meeting, to permission to print a bulky document on the office printer in exchange for some overtime work or a special assignment – that bartering thing again.

---

iii   MOOC = Massive online open course

You may have friends, acquaintances or neighbours whose skills or knowledge you can draw on.

And of course there is the internet. Find the one person who is the leading worldwide exponent of what you want to become, and get to know her or him. Such people are sure to have a website. I don't suggest you stalk someone, and if they say no, please don't keep bothering them. But there are many people out there who, with good grace, will share their experience and insights with you.

8.4 Compromises

The chances are that you will not get your renewed lifestyle exactly as you want it. There will be compromises and trade-offs.

- You might not have the funds.
- Your close family might not support the change.
- You have financial and relationship commitments that could be compromised.
- You may have to put off your dream for other reasons, like supporting a child through university.

Whatever these are, they are likely to affect you and what you want. Here you have to show a bit of maturity. On one hand, you can be purely selfish and go for your dream regardless of the consequences, or you can put your own dreams on hold because of other significant people in your life.

The solution lies somewhere in between.

The following Compromise Table, which is largely self-explanatory, can help:

Action	What would I gain?	What would I lose?	What is important?

The first three columns are relatively easy to complete. The last column may make you pause for thought. Take care to think it through thoroughly before committing yourself.

Take Action Now!

Activity 18 – Compromise Table

Write up your Compromise Table.

8.5 Building resilience

At this point I'd like to introduce you to the work of my good friend Rod Warner. Rod and I have known each other for close to thirty years. We met while working for large organisations. We both have long since left the corporate world. Rod has some amazing methodologies for understanding and increasing personal resilience. Resilience is the power-stuff that helps us through change and transition. Resilience kicks in when the going gets tough. Neither you nor I can get enough of it.

I am going to provide only a modest outline of Rod's resilience principles. I suggest you buy his acclaimed book, *The Building Resilience Handbook*, and if you get the opportunity, drop everything and attend one of his training courses. It will change your life.

This is what Rod tells us about resilience:

1. Connect to your meaning in life:
   1.1. Who are the significant people in your life? How do they provide meaning?
   1.2. Is there an important cause in your life? Does it help define you?
   1.3. Do you have a deep personal faith that gives context, meaning and direction to your life?
2. Use your unique strengths:
   2.1. By midlife you know your strengths.
   2.2. Most of the time people have pointed out your (many) weaknesses.
   2.3. You have to address weaknesses so that they don't destroy what you are trying to do, but don't let them overwhelm you.
   2.4. Your strengths will carry you through. They form the basis for your personal excellence. Understand and draw power from your strengths.
3. Maintain perspective:
   3.1. You have to think differently about negative situations and negative frames of mind.
   3.2. Try reframing the negative as an opportunity for personal growth.
   3.3. When your situation overpowers you, try doing something physical. Move to a different physical space. Go for a walk. Visit a friend. Break the negative reinforcing cycle.
4. Generate positive feelings:
   4.1. Negative emotions have an effect on your body's neurological and hormonal balance.

    4.2. Take a break.

    4.3. Get other thoughts into your mind.

    4.4. See a funny movie; laughter is helpful.
5. Be realistically optimistic:

    5.1. Choose to live with an optimistic attitude.

    5.2. See good things as permanent, and bad things as transitory.
6. Persevere by being open minded and flexible:

    6.1. Take a problem-solving approach.

    6.2. Be flexible; change your strategy and tactics when you need to.

    6.3. Don't get locked into a single all-or-nothing solution.
7. Reach out to others:

(This is probably the most surprising principle. We sometimes want to 'tough it out'. And we lose out on great support.)

    7.1. Reach out to ask for help in addressing your problem.

    7.2. Don't see asking for help as weakness; see it as a collaborative way of getting you through your problem.

    7.3. Offer help to others going through a stressful time. You will get fresh insight into your own situation and it will increase your sense of well-being.

The summary above is very limited, but it provides an insight into how to keep going through difficult times and midlife renewal is a difficult time. Get Rod's book, *Building Resilience*.[8] He explains it much better than I do and has some excellent exercises and activities for you to undertake. Make it part of your resource base. Enough said!

8.6 Summary

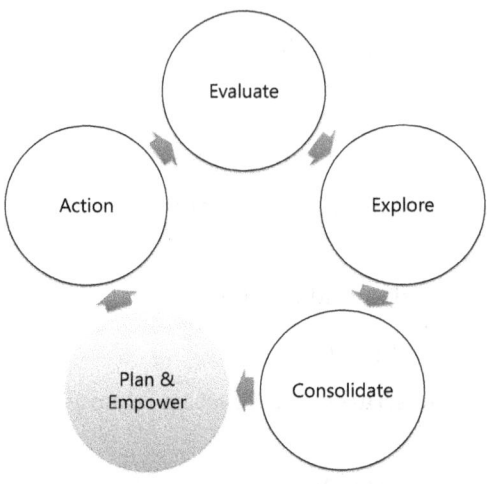

Where we are:

- You know when you are going.
- You know what you have to do.
- You have your timeline and your resources.
- You have your midlife renewal strategy clearly mapped out.

Up to this point, your work has mainly been behind the scenes. It's been about thinking, deciding and planning. You now have to move out into the open. Ideas and aspirations have to become actions!

The next section helps you realise this action and make it happen.

8.7 Case Study: Annemarie the reframer

Annemarie grew up in a patriarchal, Calvinist home. Achievement, hard work and discipline were constantly reinforced.

So when she left university and joined a large national organisation, these attributes quickly marked her as a dependable, hard worker. She delivered excellent work, on time and to specification. She ended up in a senior role in the learning and development department of the enterprise.

In the course of designing, developing and presenting learning and leadership programmes she garnered the following insights about herself.

- She was an observer. She could read situations, understand people and unravel the complexities of organisations and people. She saw things that other people missed.

- She loved learning new things and using words as a way of sharing those discernments.

- She is creative, resilient and will always find a way to land on her feet.

- She needed to look after herself. This independence meant that she did not want to rely on anyone for financial or emotional support. This was both because of her upbringing and because her marriage at a young age had failed – she was abandoned as a single mother with two small children. She did not want to be beholden to anyone.

She also realised that she was staying with this large national organisation, not because she was enjoying it, but because she needed the money. She was in the wage-slave trap. However, all was not lost. Her employer invested generously in her by way of a range of state-of-the-art learning and leadership technologies and programmes. Annemarie excelled in implementing these in the organisation and securing the desired results.

However, the organisation was going through a difficult period and large numbers of employees were being retrenched. Based on her background and her deep understanding of learning and organisations, Annemarie embarked on an internal dialogue. A what-if dialogue that went like this:

- What if I am retrenched?

- What if I no longer have the safety and security of the organisation behind me?

- What if I am alone and cast adrift?

At the same time, South Africa was going through its fundamental transition and this weighed deeply on her mind. The challenge was how to emerge from the micro and macro changes as an independent, contributing member of society at peace with herself.

In the course of her study and personal reading, Annemarie came across the following quotation from Carl Sagan:

> *"[W]e make our lives meaningful by the courage of our questions, by the depth of our answers …"*
> Carl Sagan – Visions of the 21st Century – a speech delivered in New York in 1995.

This made a deep impact on her and she resolved to ask the courageous questions and not to be terrified by the depth of the answers she discovered. What questions was she afraid to ask, while in the protective structures of a large company? How could she become more self-sufficient, more independent, but not isolated? How could she work differently in a different world, a world rapidly changing at the individual and national level? How could she make a fulfilling contribution in this very different world?

She pulled about her a web of advisers and supportive friends as she wrestled with these questions and their disturbing answers.

She knew what she had to do. She took voluntary retrenchment. There was no way back. But, as she stepped out, her erstwhile employer offered her a medium-term contract to continue doing what she had been doing while still being able to boast reduced headcount. This contract was only a short-term postponement of the inevitable. She had to clarify what her business offering would be, market her services and close sales, and master the discipline of pricing her services and delivering invoices. She set about building a successful leadership and learning business.

To date she has an enviable set of offerings and a magnificent range of clients. In her late sixties, she has a full consulting practice and has no wish to slow down. She undertakes regular recreational travel, and has time to enjoy life with her children and grandchildren. She is happier than she has ever been.

Annemarie's learnings from this experience:

- Life is not perfect, but you have to look after yourself.
- It's not about how much money you earn, but what the money does for you.
- Don't linger in an uncomfortable work situation. Do something about it, otherwise the months become years. (Remember Annie Dillard's quote in Chapter 5!)
- Asking courageous questions can help us make the right decisions.
- Don't compare who you are and what you have with other people. You are unique and you have had your own set of challenges.
- Use your core set of skills and aptitudes to rebuild a life that gratifies you.
- Give your clients the very best you can.
- Once you jump, don't look back. Make it work.
- Say no to work and clients that jar with your values.

Chapter 9

Action

When it becomes more difficult to suffer than to change ... you will change.
Robert Anthony

Midlife Renewal: Unlock the Hidden Door

This section helps to ensure that you get off to the best possible start.

9.1 The Launch

You need to launch your Midlife Renewal Strategy. That's right. Capital letters. It's your blueprint for the rest of your life.

Now, when most people think of a launch, they think of a glittering function in a large auditorium, with music and balloons and flashing lights.

Your midlife renewal strategy launch is probably going to be more low-key. The critical thing about the launch is that you have to go public. You have to 'come out'.

Going public with your midlife renewal strategy achieves three things:

- Your friends, colleagues and associates won't be nonplussed by your changed behaviours. They will understand why you are acting differently.

- The launch marks a clear break with the past. It is a symbolic jumping from the burning platform – the old change management stuff again.
- It is the symbolic action of going through the Open Door.

Here are some ideas on how to go public:

- At a family lunch, explain your decision and share what you have in mind.
- At the end of a work meeting, take a moment to share your plan with colleagues.
- If you resign from your job, explain to your boss, your peers and your subordinates why you are resigning. They may be able to provide support and assistance.
- Use social media to announce your plan. Share what you are doing on Facebook. Use Instagram or Pinterest to illustrate your new direction. Be careful to explain what you are about because so often social media postings are very cryptic and leave the reader guessing.
- At a social function with friends, engage them in conversation and let your plan drop into the exchange. They are sure to be interested and supportive.

Activity 19 – Launch your Renewed Life

The initial announcement of your renewal plans is bound to generate some interest and mild excitement. Use that energy to propel yourself forward because the novelty of your new situation will soon wither away.

The more you publicly acknowledge and commit to your plan of action, the greater the chance of success. Family, friends and colleagues modify their expectations of you, and if they have your interests at heart, which I am sure they do, they will encourage and support you.

9.2 Keeping on track

Keeping yourself on track demands effort. There are many forces, financial and emotional, that may push you back. In addition, you will have to make direction changes because some of your assumptions might not be valid, and situations and contexts may change.

Use your Gantt Chart to track progress against timeframes.

Keep in mind that your self-identity, your conception of yourself, is changing. You may have been a manager, but you are now becoming an artist. You may have been a teacher, and now you are becoming a small-scale organic farmer in your back garden. You may have had an hour's commute to work and now you work from home. The way you think about yourself, your dress and your daily rhythms, are all affected by your renewed lifestyle.

9.3 Summary

You are done!

You looked back on your life, you made an honest assessment of who you are and who you want to be, and you have taken positive, considered steps to make the rest of your life rewarding and significant.

With any change process, like the man who jumped off the burning platform into the sea, there are no guarantees. You may have followed this process meticulously, and yet there may be unintended consequences. Your earnings may be constrained, friendships may be terminated. You may have to move home or do things which you find stressful because they are unfamiliar to you. While all these events may be uncomfortable, they grow you as a person. Without trying to be fatalistic or esoteric, you are a work in progress. Some of the changes in you and the subsequent benefits and rewards may only become apparent to you much later on in the process. You have to pass through the difficult period to emerge renewed, revitalised and refocused on the other side.

Chapter 9: Action

That's it!

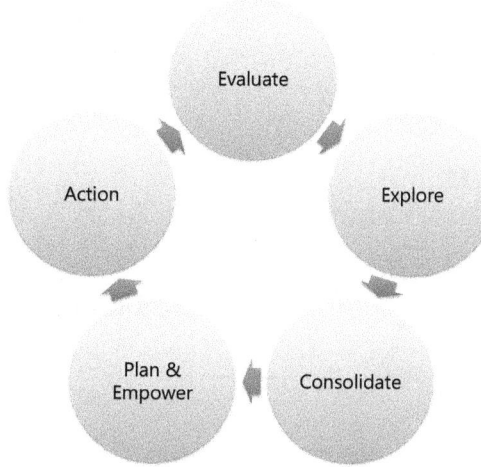

You are well on your way to a rewarding and satisfying second half of your life.

The rest of this book provides you with some journey mercies and support to guide you on your way.

Take time to savour the value and congratulate yourself on taking charge of your life. Many people go through life as slaves to factors beyond their control. You have taken charge, which puts you in a very select portion of the human population. Well done.

Activity 20 – Celebrate the New YOU

Celebrate the new person you are becoming with loved ones, family and friends. They are part of your journey.

Chapter 10

Epilogue

Death is very likely the single best invention of Life. It is Life's change agent. It clears out the old to make way for the new.
Steve Jobs

10.1 Leave something of value

I want to briefly deal with a morbid topic. Death. Yes, death; your death, my death. It's a dreadful subject. We would all prefer not to think about it. But it sneaks up on us second-halfers. Especially when we are on a path to renewal and we have so much to look forward to tomorrow, next month, next year.

Reminders come to us all the time. A neighbour of your own age dies suddenly. A well-known person dies at an age younger than you are now. Then the hard ones: a parent, a child, a close friend, a spouse or partner. We attend a funeral and we wonder ... what if I was in that coffin? You wake up one night and realise you will die. It's not a cerebral, intellectual understanding. It's a blow to the gut. One day you are going to die.

Many of the people you have admired: Gandhi, Mandela, Einstein, Hemingway – add your own list of heroes ... they are all dead. They have embarked on the last great adventure.

Maybe we are not the sort of people who morbidly obsess about our deaths. We find a way to live because the older we get, the more we realise that our renewal action comes with a certain readiness for the inevitable.

I'm not talking about religious preparedness to die. It's about living life before we die. It's not about a final frantic bucket list. Or fatuous comments about living every day as if it's your last. It's about all we have been kicking around together in this book. It's about living with dignity in the face of death. Our death may be quiet and quick, a long slow agonising cancer death, or a sudden traumatic jump-the-lights car accident. It will be the last time we go through an open door.

Dignity. Honesty. Concern for others. These are important above all else. Be the person other people would like to be.

The older we get, the wiser we become, and the happier we are. Let's show concern for the challenges and demands in the lives of others.

My dear reader, I wish you great and remarkable success. It is up to you now. Go and do it.

Warmest personal regards,

James

Index of Activities

Here are the page numbers of the activities listed in the book for easy reference.

Activity 1 - Reasons for Midlife Renewal	4
Activity 2 - Make a Journal	12
Activity 3 - Reward Yourself	51
Activity 4 - Create your Timeline	61
Activity 5 - Life Ambitions	63
Activity 6 - Adjectives that Best Describe You	67
Activity 7 - Circle of Influence	68
Activity 8 - Journal Notes	69
Activity 9 - Happiness Base	76
Activity 10 - Write up Journal	77
Activity 11 - Web Research	78
Activity 12 - Wise Folks	79
Activity 13 - Do the Work!	80
Activity 14 - Personal Business Case	90
Activity 15 - Resource Plan	93
Activity 16 - Action Plan	103
Activity 17 - Gantt Chart	104
Activity 18 - Compromise Table	107
Activity 19 - Launch your Renewed Life	117
Activity 20 - Celebrate the New YOU	119

Resources

Personal support for your own journey

For assistance in your own midlife renewal process, get in touch with me on james.forson.writer@gmail.com, or go to www.jamesforsonwriter.wordpress.com or www.jamesforson.com.

Samuel F. Mphuthi, Registered Clinical Psychologist, can be contacted in Durban at +27(0)31 332 1336 or in Pretoria at +27 (0)12 321 0506

Quotations

Some quotations in this book were taken from: http://management.simplicable.com/management/new/60-thought-provoking-change-management-quotes. *Accessed Tuesday, 15 March 2016*

The Transition Model

https://www.mindtools.com/pages/article/bridges-transition-model.htm

The three stages of transition that we go through when we experience change. While this model can help guide people through change more effectively, it's not a substitute for change management; tools such as Kotter's 8-Step Model, Lewin's Change Management Model and Bridges' model should also be considered.

The Burning Platform

http://www.connerpartners.com/frameworks-and-processes/the-real-story-of-the-burning-platform

A story to aid your understanding of the mechanics of the decision-making process.

Building Resilience

http://buildingresilience.co.za/

This is Rod Warner's Resilience page. Very definitely a must-visit. The tools to bounce back from stress at work and home. *Building Resilience*[8] is available from KR Publishing, www.kr.co.za

Kotter's 8-Step Process

http://www.kotterinternational.com/the-8-step-process-for-leading-change/

Over four decades, Dr Kotter observed countless leaders and organisations as they tried to transform or execute their strategies. He identified and extracted the success factors and combined them into a methodology, the award-winning 8-Step Process.

Lewin's Change Management Model

http://www.change-management-coach.com/kurt_lewin.html

Kurt Lewin emigrated from Germany to America during the 1930s and is recognised as the founder of social psychology which highlights his interest in the human aspect of change. His interest in groups led to research focusing on factors that influence people to change, and the three stages needed to make change successful.

The Minimalists

http://www.theminimalists.com/

Joshua Fields Millburn and Ryan Nicodemus write about living a meaningful life with less stuff. *The Minimalists* has been read by 4 million readers.

Brain Pickings

https://www.brainpickings.org/

Brain Pickings is an inventory of cross-disciplinary interestingness spanning art, science, design, history, philosophy and more.

On Being

http://onbeing.org/

On Being opens up the animated questions at the centre of human life: What does it mean to be human, and how do we want to live? It explores these questions in their richness and complexity in 21st-century lives and endeavours. *On Being* pursues wisdom and moral imagination as much as knowledge; it esteems nuance and poetry as much as fact.

Specialist Practitioners

Jackie Erasmus is an expert on organisational learning. Get in touch with her at jackie@thelearningshop.co.za

Simone le Hane is an accomplished life coach. Get in touch with her at simonelehane@change.co.za

List of Adjectives[9]

- adorable
- adventurous
- aggressive
- agreeable
- alert
- alive
- amused
- angry
- annoyed
- annoying
- anxious
- arrogant
- ashamed
- attractive
- average
- awful
- bad
- beautiful
- better
- bewildered
- black
- bloody
- blue
- blue-eyed
- blushing
- bored
- brainy
- brave
- breakable
- bright
- busy
- calm
- careful
- cautious
- charming
- cheerful
- clean
- clear
- clever
- cloudy
- clumsy
- colourful
- combative
- comfortable
- concerned
- condemned
- confused
- cooperative
- courageous
- crazy
- creepy
- crowded
- cruel
- curious
- cute
- dangerous
- dark
- dead
- defeated
- defiant
- delightful
- depressed
- determined
- different
- difficult
- disgusted
- distinct
- disturbed
- dizzy
- doubtful
- drab
- dull
- eager
- easy
- elated
- elegant
- embarrassed
- enchanting
- encouraging
- energetic
- enthusiastic
- envious
- evil
- excited
- expensive
- exuberant
- fair
- faithful
- famous
- fancy
- fantastic
- fierce
- filthy
- fine
- foolish
- fragile
- frail
- frantic
- friendly
- frightened
- funny
- gentle

- gifted
- glamorous
- gleaming
- glorious
- good
- gorgeous
- graceful
- grieving
- grotesque
- grumpy
- handsome
- happy
- healthy
- helpful
- helpless
- hilarious
- homeless
- homely
- horrible
- hungry
- hurt
- ill
- important
- impossible
- inexpensive
- innocent
- inquisitive
- itchy
- jealous
- jittery
- jolly
- joyous
- kind
- lazy
- light
- lively
- lonely
- long
- lovely
- lucky
- magnificent
- misty
- modern
- motionless
- muddy
- mushy
- mysterious
- nasty
- naughty
- nervous
- nice
- nutty
- obedient
- obnoxious
- odd
- old-fashioned
- open
- outrageous
- outstanding
- panicky
- perfect
- plain
- pleasant
- poised
- poor
- powerful
- precious
- prickly
- proud
- puzzled
- quaint
- real
- relieved
- repulsive
- rich
- scary
- selfish
- shiny
- shy
- silly
- sleepy
- smiling
- smoggy
- sore
- sparkling
- splendid
- spotless
- stormy
- strange
- stupid
- successful
- super
- talented
- tame
- tender
- tense
- terrible
- testy
- thankful
- thoughtful
- thoughtless
- tired
- tough
- troubled
- ugliest
- ugly
- uninterested
- unsightly
- unusual
- upset
- uptight
- vast
- victorious
- vivacious
- wandering
- weary
- wicked
- wide-eyed
- wild
- witty
- worried
- worrisome
- wrong
- zany
- zealous

List of Resources

Brain Pickings. (n.d.). Retrieved November, 1, 2016. https://www.brainpickings.org/

Connelly, M. 15 November 2016. *The Krut Lewin Change Management Model*. Retrieved February 21, 2018. https://www.change-management-coach.com/kurt_lewin.html

Kotter, J. 2017. *The 8-Step Process for Leading Change*. Retrieved February 21, 2018, from https://www.kotterinc.com/8-steps-process-for-leading-change/

Millburn, J.F. & Nicodemus, R. (n.d.). The Minimalists. Retrieved November, 1, 2016. https://www.theminimalists.com/

MindTools. (n.d.). *Bridges' Transition Model: Guiding People Through Change*. Retrieved November, 1, 2016, from https://www.mindtools.com/pages/article/bridges-transition-model.htm

On Being. (n.d.). Retrieved November, 1, 2016. http://onbeing.org/

References

1. William Bridges Associates. Retrieved November 1, 2016 http://www.wmbridges.com/

2. Bridges, W. 1991. *Managing transitions: making the most of change*. Reading, MA: Addison-Wesley.

3. Conner, D. 15 August 2012. *The Real story of the Burning Platform*. Retrieved November, 1, 2016. http://www.connerpartners.com/frameworks-and-processes/the-real-story-of-the-burning-platform

4. The Pennsylvania State University. 2018. *Neurons*. Retrieved February 21, 2018. https://online.science.psu.edu/bisc004_activewd001/node/1907

5. Merriam-Webster. (n.d.). Plasticity. Definition of Plasticity. Retrieved November, 1, 2016. https://www.merriam-webster.com/dictionary/plasticity

6. Bernard, S. 2010. *Neuroplasticity: Learning Physically Changes the Brain* – quote by Judy Willis. Edutopia. Retrieved November, 1, 2016. https://www.edutopia.org/neuroscience-brain-based-learning-neuroplasticity
7. Dillard, A. 2013. *The Writing Life*. New York: Harper Perennial.
8. Warner, R. 2018. *Building Resilience*. Bryanston: KR Publishing.
9. Your Dictionary. List of Adjective Words. (n.d.). Retrieved November, 1, 2016. http://grammar.yourdictionary.com/parts-of-speech/adjectives/list-of-adjective-words.html